Skinny Kid

From The

Green Grass

Frank Borrelli

ISBN: ISBN-13: 978-1544180311

ISBN-10: 1544180314

This is a true story.
Only a few names have been changed to protect their privacy.

Published in the United States of America

Bootstrap Publishing
www.Bootstrappublishing.net
mkd@bootstrappublishing.net
Rochester, New York

DEDICATIONS

To my wife, Jeannie

To all of those that have brought joy and love into my life, and there have been many, I am eternally grateful.
For all that have brought sorrow, I forgive you.

In memory of Mr. Arnold B. Swift, Principal of Jefferson High school. Mr. Swift was the most underrated educator of his time. I personally believe that he was the best educator I have ever met.

The purpose of this book was to point out to young people that when the person reaches "the age of reason" that person is responsible for their own actions.

This is in my own words.

This book is not meant to have family follow in my footsteps. I believe that each of us is 100% responsible for what we are to become and what we are to achieve. Those were other times and I believe that I could have whined and pouted or I could have attacked. Retreat, regardless for what reason, is more difficult than attacking.

I thank my dad for his teaching and being a great role model. I always knew my dad had my back. I thank all my surrogate mothers for teaching me respect and values, and above all various Italian old-world customs. Plus, let us not forget the value of a "magic mirror." This mantra was given to me by Ange Marcone a friend and role model. Another WWII POW that bailed out over Italy in 1944. *Mirror! Mirror! on the wall I am the tallest of them all.*

I know I have made my share of mistakes but, "I did it my way." Now, to all of you that I love, "do it your way."

Many thanks to the family for their support especially Ashley and Nicole for their constant compliments.

After reviewing the proofs of this book over the past several months and correcting the mistakes not caught by various "editors," I think I may have gone into the editing business. For all my family and friends; I do hope you can forgive my grammar and appreciate my thoughts to leave my great grandchildren on their ancestry. Most of all, I hope that you enjoy and forgive my amateur attempt at being an author, for I did feel an act of "love" while thinking of you all.

Cia Bambinos

Positive Vibes

"I want you to know how important a part you and Jeannie played in my life journey, for without you I wouldn't be where I am today. You gave a wild kid who just came home from two years in Paris a chance to explore and grow in the world of travel and supported me in my career growth. When I think of my time at Borrelli Travel in the Lincoln concourse I always smile."

- Kathleen Muldermans

"Well sir, YOU have a nice little read here on your hands. I'm serious, you've had an interesting life, and I've only read the first chapter! You really are blessed Frank, (but I'm sure I'm not telling you anything you don't already know).

- Christie Stacy

"Mr. Frank Borrelli, author, inspirational personality, encourager and friend to many! ... Your story is one of hope and resilience... of opportunity and self-correction."

- Suzanne Van Gombos

"This book grabs hold of you from the first page. I want to know about Frank and his experiences. To read about what life was like back in the 40's and 50's left me feeling sad that we no longer have the pride or the closeness this great generation experienced. Frank goes into detail of his experiences and makes you almost feel like you are living his life. This is a fascinating book that I just can't put down."

- Peggy Page

REFERENCES

"Honore de Balzac," – the 'de' was added by him to show someone with a title – a French writer. Maybe the first to use "Autres temps in literature," original proverb can mean:

Autres temps, autres moeurs

1. other days-other ways
2. other times-other customs
3. other times-other manners
4. other times-other countries

"Honore" was a nineteenth-century French novelist and playwright. He wrote many plays and novels. He was born in 1799 and died in 1850. His many novels and plays (over 100) were printed in a collection which represented a panorama of French life in the years after the fall of Napoleon. Apparently, this collection contained reference to Autres temps-autres moeurs.

This was also used most recently by the Dean of Oxford University to rebuke a few Mandela Rhodes scholarships; student activists. The activists had wanted to erase Mr. Rhodes' presence on campus because of slave ownership.

"C'est la vie," literally, this is life. English translation "shit happens" or my interpretation "eh, that's life" or "eh, so be it".

"Pearl Mesta," the "hostess with the mostest" she was a diplomat; Ambassador to Luxembourg. When I mentioned Pearl, it was "we were the Pearl Mesta of our time." We were the only one of our friends to invite someone almost every weekend. It seemed that so many of the couples we ran with were all not willing or felt that their house was not big enough.

"For every negative, there is a positive"

While I was in the hospital, an eighteen-year-old Marine in the next bed was shot right through his face in combat. When I showed concern, his reply was "no problem, **the negative is…** I will have a dimple, and when it heals, **the positive is…** I will get the hell out of here before I get killed."

OMG- "Oh my God!"

Our 10th Annual Thanksgiving Eve
Theme: What to be thankful for.
Dinner with the grandchildren.
November 2016

Chapter I

It All Started Long Before I Was Born.

It all started long before I was born. Ancestry speaks a loud voice in our genes. Let's start at the turn of the century, Borrelli – Bovenzi (died 1944) Grandpa Borrelli born 1872 Grampa Frank Borrelli and Grandma Theresa Bovenzi. My Dad Frank P Borrelli Born 1910 and My Mother Josephine Cartisano Born 1911.

1931-1935

And the winner is Francis Borrelli!

Born Francis Borrelli; (September 7, 1931) and at the ripe age of two, I won a beauty contest at the N.Y. State Fair. Thus, my family received two tickets to Hollywood for a guest appearance in an "our gang" comedy movie. My father and his cronies entered me, and my mother wanted no part in it. After winning, she turned the page and wanted one of the tickets, so my father tore them all up, and nobody went. Oh well, there went my chance at stardom.

While growing up, I learned of this story from two local bowling stars, their names; Frank Delconte and Marky Chafel. Both Frank and Marky accompanied my father to Syracuse for the fair. It's amazing how much can be remembered from age four, during The Big Depression of the 1930's.

We lived in a two-story house on Romeyn Street, with outside stairs leading to our apartment. Dad was working, or maybe out of town, I am not exactly sure but I remember mom going up those

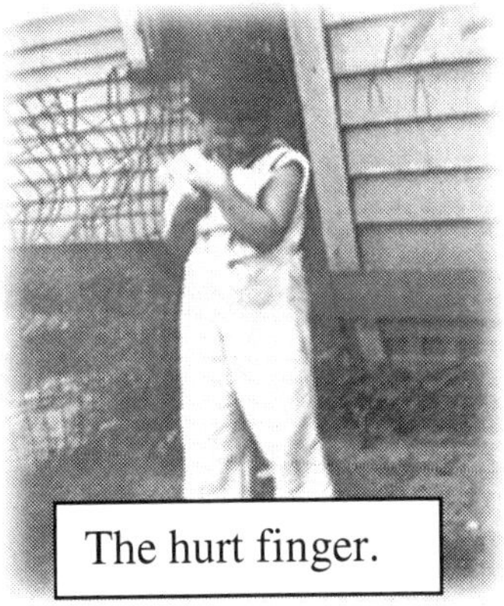

The hurt finger.

stairs with her "friend." I was left outside to play in the yard. I must have been inquisitive and put my finger in an old salt shaker bottle. While trying to get my finger out, I started to cry, and called for my mother. After a time, she finally heard me and came to the door, only to holler at me, telling me to take my finger out of the old salt shaker bottle.

Luckily, I was an intelligent four-year-old. I found a large stone and smashed the glass shaker along with a part of my finger. Blood and tears followed, and the bottle left a small scar on my finger as proof.

My Grandmother, Mother and me.

Another time, I wanted to crawl in bed with my mother. She did not want to be bothered, so the sheets were arranged so I was only on top of the sheets and below a blanket. So much for "motherly love!" Somehow, I don't remember my dad being around. I remember my mother's brother coming home from a tour with the CCC camp. This program introduced by FDR, is no longer taught in schools. President Roosevelt started this military type of organization during the depression for all unemployed Americans. As part of the program, they built roads and parks around the country. Also, known as the "Civilian Conservation Corp," their uniforms resemble that of the Army's. Some of the largest parks in the USA were built by these men.

> **Pair Shares Child, Balks at Reunion**
>
> While spurning a reconciliation, Frank J. Borrelli, 23 Montrose Street, and his estranged wife, Mrs. Josephine M. Borrelli, 78 Grape Street, yesterday with the aid of Supreme Court Justice James P. B. Duffy reached an amicable agreement on custody of their 5-year-old son, Frank Jr.
>
> Under Justice Duffy's ruling, reported satisfactory by attorneys for both sides, Borrelli is to have custody of his son from Monday through Friday each week and the boy will be with his mother Saturdays and Sundays. Mrs. Borrelli started habeas corpus proceedings last week to regain custody of her son, whom she claimed was "spirited away" in an automobile by her husband while the youngster was playing on the porch of her home, July 5. The husband maintained the boy wished to accompany him. Under a previous arrangement out of court, the child passed part of each week with each parent, alternating weekends. The new agreement yesterday avoided a lengthy court proceeding. Husband and wife both have jobs and live at the homes of their parents.

Finally, in 1934 my mother and I moved in with her mother, my grandmother. Apparently, a few years prior, her husband was killed in Italy. He was shot coming out of a bank in Reggio Calabria. They say he was vying for the head of an organization called "Mano Nero" (Black Hand). Therefore, my Grandmother Maggie was a widow. (I found out today that Maggie's name was Domenica this means Sunday). She felt that she should have an Americanized name. Wanting to Americanize her name Maggie chose Margaret as her name. (Hence the Maggie, short for Margaret).While living with her, on one occasion while my mother was giving me a bath; "Jim" gave me a small motor boat to keep me busy while taking baths. I am certain that he put an aspirin in the motor spot and it produced bubbles that propelled the boat. This "Jim" character, for some reason I did not like.

A few days later, my dog and I were playing in the front yard at 82 Grape Street. It seemed like any other day, until a car pulled up on the wrong side of the street. My father jumped out, grabbed me, left the dog, and threw me in the car. I'll never forget bumping my head on the way in. He kidnapped me, he was only twenty-five years old, I was still four. I was hidden at my aunt's house until the court decided to give my father custody. I guess my mother did not fight too hard to keep me. Recently I subscribed to Archives of the Rochester Newspaper, Democrat and Chronicle.

It was so comforting to have all the stories dad told me come to life and find that he was "spot on." This incident was in the news for three days; in fact, dad was very kind compared to what went on. He must have been arrested because a Habeas Corpus was issued. Definition is that "a person incarcerated comes before a Judge and pleads their case to be let out of jail." What I was unaware of, was that she was granted weekend visitation. She did not show up for twenty years.

A New Life Begins

My father and I moved in with Grandpa and Grandma Borrelli, and Aunt Teresa, "the single sister." This address was 44 Fulton Ave, and within weeks we all moved to 21 Montrose Street.

There were maybe fifty houses on the street, one school house (School #6) and a broom factory. Forty-seven of these houses were first generation Italians, the other three were American families. The Americans were Mr. and Mrs. Jeff, Mrs. Roth, and Mr. and Mrs. Hudson. This is important because in those days, there were only two types of people, Italians, and Americans.

Within a year, I had no less than ten surrogate mothers. Mama Rosie, Madeleine, Mrs. Roth, Mrs. Carbone, Mrs. Hudson, Mrs. Valente and one they called "Mussolini" (another Borrelli). This gent's real name was Domenic Borrelli, he loved Benito Mussolini, the dictator from the old country. To all, I was the "little curly head kid with no mother."

The third from the left is my grandfather Cartisano, he was killed in Calabria Italy in 1927.

I remember sitting on the porch of Mr. Swazie, he was confined to a wheel chair due to injuries suffered serving during WW1. For hours, he would tell me stories of the Great War, and I considered Louie my friend. His son Dante was handsome, and known as the "Don Juan" of his generation.

One thing I remember for sure was that there were no "old people." All these people were my friends. My grandfather and grandmother included in my daily life. And when someone died they were laid out in your living room or bed room as was the case in my house.

My only regrets were that I did not get to see my uncle Peter before he died in a Veterans Hospital of wounds suffered in WW1.

My grandma had health problems. She was comical to a ten-year-old. In the middle of the night, the whole ceiling above her head tore away from the lath and came down on her. [But only above her head came down] the rest of the room remained intact. OMG she began to wail she was convinced it was an omen or some curse. Also, I remember her teeth or lack of them caused her to eat everything mashed or softened.

Grandpa was different. He had a handle bar mustache and went to work every day with a heavy broom with a steel knife like object at the top of the broom. He oversaw maintaining a seven-mile set of tracks on both sides of Lake Ave. One set going north to the Beach on Lake Ontario and the south bound on the street returning. The pick at the end of the broom was to clear ice or residue off the tracks if any. The broom was to clear any debris from the street car tracks and surrounding area. I loved my grand pa, Italian tobacco and all.

Grampa Borrelli in his favorite chair.

Many days grandpa would grab me by the hand and take me to work for the day. After arriving at the beach, he would buy me Abbots famous frozen custard. Nonno Joe taught me how to use tools and do brick and mortar work. In those days, a mason also did carpentry, some electric and any work that prevented the craftsman from completing the job. Now a-days a mason will stop and wait for other tradesmen to do their thing and not allow anyone to encroach on their work. Nonno Joe was good company for Grandpa, seeing that they both spoke a dialect of Italian. Nonno Joe was a "boarder" he lived with my Grandpa and Dad until his death in 1955.

1936-1944: LEARNING TO LIVE WITH DIVORCE

This was the beginning of living without a mother. Without knowing what to call it, (divorce) and we became a single parent family.

I was enrolled in a catholic school St. Anthony of Padua. All my little friends from Montrose St. and surrounding streets went to # 6 school. By this time, about 1940 we moved up to 51 Montrose. This was a neat house, directly in front of the Broom Factory and across the street from #6 school. Within four years, I knew all the mechanics involved in the making of a broom. We learned how to smoke the corn stalks. Now, this was something else, get a bunch of the ends of the stalk, climb the gutter pipes of # 6 school and stay up in the corner of the roof and try to smoke. Life in the old days.

Another advantage of living near the Broom Factory, I worked there from about eleven to fourteen, we were born with a work permit in those days. When no one was around, I would cut new broom handles to a specific length and dip paint various colors including red, white and blue swirl.... these were needed to play Stick Ball. New York and Boston were the only cities that played this game. Manhole covers were used for home and second plate. Light pole on the right was first base and on the left, was third base. The ball was the size of tennis ball, and no gloves, pitcher would one, bounce the ball towards the batter. The rest was pure baseball. I also thought that the ball was hard to hit, until I tried Andrew and Nicholas at bat on our tennis court. They literally killed the ball. "Autres temps." This was a different time and a different place and time.

Another of our great "baseball" games were "against the steps" As few as two can play my son Frank and I later would play for hours in the back yard using the cellar block. Number six school had seven steps in front of the school. At the top of the steps was a huge platform of concrete where kids would stay and wait for the school bell to ring and open the door for class to begin.

Step ball positions were simple and two kids usually, played one on one. A team had two fielders or two fielders and a "catcher." The catcher patrolled that large platform at the top of the steps and one infielder about ten feet in front of the steps. The outfielder would be in the street and get the high long ones. Markers were set for a single, double etc. Of course, the opposing team would "be at bat" throw the tennis ball at the steps and aim for the corners of the steps…this would get the ball to travel far and high. Miss that hot spot and you get a grounder. My next-door neighbor Mario was hit by a car and seriously injured while playing the outfield in the street. We had our share of impatient drivers then also.

Another great game was pitching baseball cards against a step. One to four of us would get our cards that we got free when we bought bubble gum. Line up at the curb and pitch the card like a Frisbee to the step, if we were four, start from left to right. Closest to the step was the winner he got the first shot at winning. Closer than the closest was a "Hubbard." A "Hubbard" was a card that hit the step and the top of the card leaned up against the step like a ladder. Now the closest one collects all cards and heaves them up in the air. All that come-up heads he gets to keep. This is continued from the leader to the 2nd closest etc. Any remaining cards start over from the number one guy. God, I wish I still had those cards. They would be worth a fortune now. No cards? Pitch pennies. Pennies were great to put on the street car tracks. Once the street car ran over a penny it was crushed like an ornament or rarity.

Now of our young lives, we were learning "street stuff." We hated the Japanese and Germans. Our brothers and fathers and cousins were getting killed by these awful people. I believe in war, you must learn to hate your opponent this I know now first hand. My very dear friend Sam Dauria was so lucky. He lived next door to # 6 school; next to our tackle football field. (He later became the quarter back and I was the center on our Edgerton Park Football team).

Sam had a brother, mother, sister and a BB rifle, a Red Rider one. Also, he had a dog called "Skipper." We trained the dog to react to the chant, "Dirty Jap." Whenever Skipper heard this he started to scratch dig a hole. As we increased our chant faster, Skipper would dig the hole deeper and deeper. This is how we would dig some of our holes for "Marbles." Another game pitching marbles into the hole or at least closest, so you got first shot with your thumb to roll it into the hole for a keeper.

I loved that street and unfortunately had to go to St. Anthony's a two-mile walk. You haven't lived until you walked to school. Friendships were formed during these walks, games were played, coming to and from school. Returning, if you had a penny or two we stopped at Di Martino's Meat Market and Grocery Store to purchase a candy bar.

The greatest fun was playing "king of the Royal Mountain." Sidewalks were always plowed at least once a day in the winter. I think our winters were more severe back then. Plows were pulled by a team of horses. All snow was "thrown" between the sidewalk and curb. To this mass was added all the snow from the street between the two was formed large "mountains" of snow. A walk on top of these mountains were a trip up and slide down sometime when you consider a third element. The individual driveways were in where the lucky families with a car lived. These people added more snow to our mountains.

The king ruled the top until someone pulled or shoved them off their "mountain." Did some kids fall into the street? Yes! And were there injuries? Yes! Did we have fun? Heck yes! Were the nuns angry when you came to school with loads of wet snow on your clothing, did you have to clean up the mess? Yes, and sometimes some little fisticuffs took place, and a little blood was mixed with the snow.

Another great "sport" was to go on raiding parties at night. Every home had an Italian garden for blocks around. The Great War (WW1) was over but now was (WW2) and rationing was the way of life. The war effort needed food and petrol, so just about everything was in short supply.

These first-generation Italians were from an Agrarian culture, in "the Old Country" they all had gardens and still do. We would dress like our big brothers did in the war, no noise, blacken your face and crawl into the yards. OMG, fresh carrots, cucumbers, tomatoes, celery; a couple yards had apple, peach and cherry trees. Man, we had none of this at home. If it was available in the stores, we could not afford it.

All the fun and games were great and I got along with my friends very well. All their mothers were very generous. I was like an additional child of theirs. But school sometime presented a problem. If we were told to bring our mother to school, my canned remark was that I was unable to because she was dead. There was no kindergarten so at age a few days shy of five, I was put into the first grade. All the other boys were bigger and older. I held my own and the older kids would make me fight the older chubbier kids that were more student instead of athletes. Stupid and nasty and I regretted that part of school.

And grade two, I remember having a boil on my knee and the sister lanced it at noon and put salve on it. I remember that and had a special place for her. In fourth grade one of the older kids about four years older would make small paper cut outs and make them dance. He would run his comb through his hair and then place the comb above the paper doll, the static electricity would cause the doll to rise and fall. Hello, you know he never made it to the 6th grade and quit school. I remember in the 5th grade Sr. Paulinis had a sign around the clock on the wall. Lost time is never found again, another mantra.

Of course, I could not go home for lunch. So, I walked a few blocks to Roncones Restaurant. This was the greatest. Gilda and her sisters ran the restaurant. Gilda's father owned the business and she, being single, he gave her the restaurant and he survived with the bar only. More surrogate mothers, and my Aunt Teresa worked at the restaurant so, all was cool. I was one of the family.

ENTER "HELEN" INTO MY LIFE

We were still living with Grandpa Borrelli, when my dad introduced me to Helen. Dad informed me that we were moving to Ambrose Street a few blocks away. I am not sure what the exact explanation was for Helen. After a time, I "got the picture." Dad had gotten married and I had a "step mother" whatever that meant.

Helen was not a welcomed guest. At first, I was rebellious and my favorite nasty was, "you cannot tell me what to do, you are not my mother." The positive side (again my mantra) was that she could teach me a few things. She was a high school graduate, and was intelligent. Some of the things I learned from her I am still using to this day. Helen taught me how to keep a budget and a budget book weekly before I even spent a penny; I put away for my expenses and entertainment and a small amount in a savings account. She also taught me how to ride a horse. No one, but no one, in or near our neighborhood had a clue how to ride a horse.

Helen's grandfather owned many acres on Elmwood Ave. Two riding academies rented land from Grampa Jones. One was Von Lambach and the other one was Elmwood Riding Academy. We would go to these places on a Saturday and ride some on the bridle trails. As a ten-year-old this was a super big deal.

Saraiki-White Snow
Emperor Hirohito's horse.

I thought I was a real (Tom Mix the movie star.)

Many years later while in a Japanese Military Hospital recovering from burns to my legs we were given a day trip. A few ambulatory patients were taken to the former Emperor's Royal Palace and Gardens. Horses have a high spot in Japanese culture almost a religious meaning. Emperor Hirohito was never seen except on one of his Stallions. One was named Hotsu Shimo (First Frost), The other was named Sirayuki (White Snow). We could ride one of the many horses. I was lucky to get one of the white stallions. He was much wiser than I, this horse knew I was not an experienced rider, even if I thought so. He kept running next to a fence to scrape me off also by turning his head to the left tried biting me. Finally, I gave him the reins and let him proceed to the barns. That was the end of my cowboy days. We must keep in mind, this was 1950 only five years since the end of the war. We occupied both

Japan and Germany; we controlled all the countries. This occupation included all treasures and constabulary duties.

After six months, we decided to move in with Grandpa Borrelli at 51 Montrose St., Helen was a kind person and fit in very well with all the older Italian Speaking Ladies. This was a weird thing; Helen would take Grandma Rosie to the local Harts store to shop for the few things that were available. Rationing was in force at that time, and Helen was the Italian ladies advocate and she made sure that these ladies got their fair share. But there were times that some Italian speaking ladies from a few streets over would say something vulgar towards the "Americano," the ladies would be shocked when Helen made it known that she understood what they were saying. I never called Helen mother or mom. My first letter from Korea for some reason I felt differently and addressed the letter to Dear Mom and Dad. War will do that to you.

At 5th Grade I also became an Altar Boy I still remember some of the Latin. At Mass, we usually had two Altar Boys. We would walk in front of the Priest and open for him to stand in the middle. This would be at the foot of the Altar he would say the prayers in Latin and we would respond also in Latin. The Priest would make the sign of the cross and say "in nonmine Patris et Feili et Spiritus Santi Amen."

In the name of the father, the son, and the Holy Ghost [now it's the Holy Spirit}

Priest: Introbo ad atare Dei
[I will go to the Altar of God]
Server: Ad Diem qui laetificat juventuitem meam
[To God the joy of my youth]

Years later I experienced a very sad moment. While on a troop ship on my way to Korea, our Chaplin was to say Sunday Mass. He asked if there were any ex-altar Boys to assist in the mass. I told him I was, but I was a little rusty with the Latin. He refused my offer. This hurt because I could have read the responses from the missal prayer book. Times have changed, now the Mass is in English. Shake it off, I just want to get this year over with and make it home.

In the 8th grade I made the baseball team. Hey right field, I hoped no one hit it there. I think I made the throw to the 2nd base man on a couple of bounces. One thing we all did and I continued to do this till I was fifty years old, and playing slow pitch. We always made the sign of the cross in the sand next to the plate. This was fast pitch and we did have a great pitcher. I think he was maybe fifteen or sixteen and in the 8th grade and never made it to high school. It is sad so many kids without guidance. His older brother was the friend of my dad that was killed with the fireworks.

Also in the 8th grade Nick Borrelli, no relation and Gigi went to the Franciscans. Pressure was put on me to go. My dad said no. 12-year-old kids cannot make that kind of call. Father Nick would come home once a year with his robe as a Monk and played hard ball. He was a great ball player. He left the Monastery and married and moved to Leroy. He was mayor of Leroy for many years.

When Notre Dame High School needed a principal, and could not afford one, Nick took the job for no pay. Today, if you look at the archives in the Democrat and Chronicle, in his day as Mayor, he was in the paper almost weekly.

Another "memory" for Memorial Day, all schools marched in the parade. A required dress code was white shirts and blue pants for the boys. Well, I did not have a white shirt so Aunt Teresa came up with light beige. When I arrived at school, I thought it was the end of the world. Sister put me in the middle of the pack. Regardless of size I was like a little runt in the middle. Chalk up another one for the poor kid without a mother.

But one happy day in June we were taken to Sea Breeze Amusement Park. Admission to the rides was one Coca Cola bottle cap, or five cents. While in the "Spooky" House [where all is black as toast] I put my arm around the prettiest girl in the class. I was still eleven years old and got my first kiss and my second I think. She was thirteen, and five years later almost was killed when struck by an auto. I haven't seen her since. I believe I went into the service shortly after the accident.

At my age now, I feel so sorry that all our children know very little of our Great Country. I think all born in my time were privy to know President Franklin Delano Roosevelt and his programs, during the great Depression. And in WW2 he was magnificent. Schools no longer teach these things in history. And if you are not a history major, you may never know.

Here are a few things that we were a part of. Even to mention these give me the chills. These are some of the joys of our youth. Remember now, we didn't have a TV or an iPhone. Also, my Mantra is that "for everything negative, there will be a positive." So, the outcome of most of these negatives had a great positive.

1. The Great Depression. Franklin [or FDR as he was called] Roosevelt, gave us great guidance through the great depression. Such as the NRA the National Recovery Program.

2. The FDIC to strengthen the banks. This protected all of us against bank failure.

3. Civil work program was also known as the CCC program." Civilian Conversation Corps," this program was for the unemployed. Most of our National parks were built by these "troops" boy can we use this today!

4. Fair labor standards; put a stop to the hiring of children. This was a big problem at that time; getting these young children and pay them pennies on the dollar.

5. He abolished prohibition. Hooray!

6. His great speeches during WWII. No one ever missed the noon news. Everyone always waited for the end. You knew when it was ended. "It's not over till the fat lady sings." This was Kate Smith she ended all programs with the song God Bless America. She also led the country in song daily. Mostly patriotic, bring the boys back home. Frank Sinatra claims that she was the best voice of her time. We all knew her and loved her. WW2 was from Dec.8, 1941 to Aug. 15, 1945 VJ day. [Victory in Japan.}

7. The war! Every family had someone in the service. Brother, sister, uncle, father.

8. We remember the houses with the Gold star in the window for a service person on duty. We had one for Uncle Louis in our window. "Grandma" next door had a string of four stars, four sons in the Navy. All my aunts had at least one son in the service. So, I had four cousins that were my heroes. Some gave me their old baseball jerseys when they left. A little large for me but I loved them. They also brought back some souvenirs for me.... The rules were that brothers could not serve together on the same ship. This was a result of a large ship either a Battleship or a Carrier, had five brothers aboard, the Sullivan Brothers. The ship was destroyed and the brothers all died. Rules have since been changed to include all branches of the service

9. Who can ever forget VJ day? August 14,1945 WOW the war was over. Every city in the world celebrated. The Axis Powers, Germany, Japan, and unfortunately some of Italy did not celebrate.

The Kiss

Any one near Sarasota Fl., please go to Sarasota Beach. There is a larger than life statue of the most famous picture taken in NYC on that day. It is a sailor kissing a nurse; "the kiss" became famous. The nurse was Greta Zimmer a twenty-one-year-old dental hygienist. Both parents were killed in the Holocaust because they were Jewish. But Greta made it to the USA at age fifteen. Greta died on September 10, 2016 at the age of ninety-one. The Sailor's name was George Mendoza. This was truly a "symbol of joy." This was just a highly spontaneous happening that took over the whole USA.

We in Rochester were just as festive. I was still only thirteen years old and went to Main Street…The plan was to kiss all girls walking. I am not sure I kissed a girl yet but wow…. Then some idiot broke a five and dime store window. I am not sure it was on purpose, but the window was loaded with hundreds of bangle bracelets. These were thin look like silver bracelets and the point was to wear maybe a dozen or so. Well I put about fifty in my pockets and every girl I kissed I gave one to. The good thing was that we meet some pretty girls that lived about ten blocks away from Edgerton Park.

They lived on Avery and McNaughton St. To this day, we are good friends. On a visit, later while sitting on one girl's porch I noticed a few rooms un occupied yet there was a light still lit in the house. Man, when I left a room at my house I had to turn the light off. This was a waste of money that we did not have.

I never could forget that. That was my first encounter with the "rich."

A few other things you shall never see. Al's Stand for the great Lemonade or Lemon Ice, A penny a cone and later five cents a cone.

And across the street was the "Green Grass" This was known only to us at Edgerton Park. It was a large triangle of grass dividing the 3 streets. Here we played and invented slow pitch. Not much room so we played lefty, righty. Bat the opposite way and pitch lob ball. There were 6 baseball fields in Edgerton Park, but we were not allowed to go on the fields because there were Industrial leagues at 6 pm. So, ground keepers would be through marking and grooming the fields at 10 am and just guard and smoke cigarettes until game times. That's life.

Today August 21, 2016

Today I visited my old neighborhood. I wanted to share all the good things I remembered with my readers and family. My first stop was Montrose Street. It is no longer a two-way street, but a one way from Plymouth Ave. Sealtest Dairy has taken over the whole block from Fulton Ave to Plymouth Ave. This is where we went to in the afternoon to get the ice that the drivers had left over. Was a milkmen way back then called drivers or jockeys? They delivered milk by horse and buggy. There was no gasoline through World War II. My house and the broom factory are long gone. Saint Anthony church replaced both buildings. The school for St. Anthony was built where number six school was.

No more porches remain on the houses. Gone are all the beautiful rails and steps with the great rocking chairs and gliders. All houses have an extra room built in front of the structure. All that remains of my childhood; is "home plate," the man hole cover and the light pole for third base. I took photos of the starkness of the street that I share in this book.

Next, I drove to Saratoga and turned right. Mary's Linen shop is now an apartment (Mary was one of my surrogate mothers). Next Jean's uncle Rocky's store is no more. The Edgerton bowling alley and bar is all boarded up. I parked at the "Green Grass "on the Saratoga side. Across the street is Al's stand the other two sides of the green grass are both called Bloss St. I never took time to notice this. Bloss street was laid out around the start of the 20th century. This part was over 100 yards wide so it was determined that a plot of land with two-foot curbing be landscaped in the middle of the street. This triangle had homes on the south side and a few buildings on the north side. Inside the North side for acres was Edgerton Park named after former Rochester Mayor Hiram Edgerton. There is no longer an Edgerton Park but an Edgerton Recreation Center

Al's stand is smaller than I remembered OMG! I was weirded out, it is overwhelmed by the house Al and family lived in. Next, I walked the perimeter of the green grass, while Jean waited in the car. I had such a weird feeling with tears in my eyes I heard George Delucia the "Mayor," Joe "Snail" Nacca, Jerry Peters, Anthony "Mentels" Mentesano, Billy Benedict [the only non-Italian in the bunch].

I stopped in front of the former house of John Vito. Listening for more familiar voices I heard Sonny Giuliano and remember a time while playing a game of cards called Brisco; an Italian game that allows one to talk almost to the point of legal cheating. A bird flew by and let go of a whole bunch of gook onto his chest; while he was giving a signal across his chest. The signal was an act of cheating; telling his partner to come in "Hearts."

Al's Stands,
it seems so much smaller.

My biggest disappointment was to see all the trees planted in the last sixty years on our baseball field. They are gorgeous and the grass is so beautiful now. But there is no bench or anywhere one could lay down with ten or twelve friends and solve all the problems of the day. Above all we knew every Italian name in any sport. We would listen to the portable radio and heard when the Montreal Royal team had a great Italian catcher named Roy Campenela. Then we went to a Red Wing game against Montreal and saw Campenela play. Roy was black. We loved him anyway.

Th Green Grass

As I walked to my car I noticed a beer can and a few soda bottles thrown on the green grass. This was as if someone stabbed the memory of all those guys mentioned. This was hallowed ground "one should never mess in a place you live in." When I returned from the service there was no more fast pitch only slow pitch. "The game we know we invented."

How about going to "Sister Woods" for Turtles and Pollywogs? Sister Woods was behind Aquinas. We could not see the school from the woods and knew nothing about the school. We were about ten years old. We walked to Dewey Ave. Through the Arbia family yard, downhill to the subway tracks. Follow the tracks north to a place called "sister woods." I doubt if the kids that go there today are aware of its existence. I also am sure that it's no longer called "sister woods."

How about our pro basketball team, the Rochester Royals? We never ever missed a game of any kind at the Sports Arena. Boxing, Wrestling, Big Bands, you name it.... Of course, we never had to pay some of us had our favorite tool hidden nearby to pry or force the door open. If this was a sellout game, adults paid us a dollar to sneak them into the game. Sometimes we had to enter by crawling over the ceiling in the player's room. But the best thing in the world was if the arena was set up for boxing the ring would be on the court and the royals would come to our Building 6 to practice.

Occasionally if the winter was severe a few players did not show up. I wish I could say I checked Fuzzy Lavene here, but I did pass him an out of bounds ball. But my dear friend Joseph Coccia did go one on one with Fuzzy. Joe was about 6 ft. and an excellent basketball player.

The Rochester Royals, now the Sacramento Kings. Picture this; to gain entrance it would cost at least $100.00…. Champion Game would cost hundreds.

The years of 1944 to 1948, the skinny kid did the following impossible things. Before each game, I would go to the Sports Arena and get a stack of game programs from the front office. From seven to eight o'clock, I would huckster programs to fans. "programs here, get your program here. "Ya can't tell a player without a program." Then from eight pm to ten pm I would sell Coca Cola. A case of 24 bottles and a handful of cups…. For a thirteen-year-old, these bottles were heavy going up and down the steps. I always made sure I passed the players bench (I can hear Dutch Garfinkel from Brooklyn to this day)." See, I passed it to Soyvay and Soyvay, passed it to Davis and so on. The name was Cervie, but imagine how it came out in Brooklynese. I never knew what or where was Brooklyn, but it sure was a treat.

The greatest thing in the world, probably the greatest thing ever, one night Les Harrison came out to the lobby and asked if I wanted to be the water boy for the night. I was loaded up with water and packages of gum. Players chewed gum like crazy. When the night was over, Les gave me gum and five cents.

After about three years the bigger kids and adults caught on that basketball was here to stay. Not a problem we moved on and with the help of Pat Tallini, we had a few crowbars hidden in the weeds outside. Pat taught us how to pry open a few of the emergency exits. We could sneak into every attraction. That was held in the Sports Arena. From basketball to wrestling, boxing, the Negro League, of which I knew all of them.... Puggy Bell, Zack Clayton, Dolly King and many more. Also, the "Big Bands." We never missed a thing. Another Autres-temps; Big time rivalry and play off.... Rochester Royals vs. the Ft. Wayne Zollner Pistons. Dozens of well-dressed men outside trying to get in and the game was sold out by seven o'clock pm...." Hay mister, want to see the game for a dollar?" "yea kid." "here is the plan, the exit doors are guarded, but we can get you in from the city garage, over the top of the rafters, over the players dressing rooms, then into the Arena. "done deal."

Man, I challenge any of the generation since, to beat that. After all, we owned the park and there was absolutely nothing that went on in Edgerton Park that we could not sneak into.

We worshiped real heroes, Jonas Salk found a cure for Polio for one. My next-door neighbor, Grandma Rosie's daughter had Polio. Colin Kelly our first Air Ace, friends that had brothers in the OSS. These guys jumped behind German lines and rid themselves of their Uniform and fell into the civilian populace. Once you get rid of the uniform if caught you are executed as a spy. How about Albert Einstein the atom? I personally saw the devastation of Nagasaki. While on a Hospital train to Nogoya Hospital we passed through Nagasaki where the second bomb hit. Only a few sticks were left standing.

Six School Gang

1944-1948: Joining a gang

An explanation is needed now. A gang was not a bad word in those days, it really was only a means of identity. But there was a great feeling of camaraderie and the learning to protect your friends back. Occasionally the rivalry would get a little testy, but not like today, afterwards you usually shook hands with each other.

We were the" # 6 school Gang," or "Costar St. Gang." Later after about thirteen or fourteen you began to separate. Most of us went to the Edgerton Park Gang some went to Jones Park. And some went to the Library.

A list of some westside Gangs were:
30 School Gang
The Jones Park
The Brown Square
The Dutch Town
The Spencer Street
The Parkway
The Bulls Head

Next to make your identity known, you were either from the westside or eastside. Rochester is one of a few cities to be divided by a river. The Genesee River divides the city into the westside and East side. "And never the twain shall meet." We were the westside.

Eastsiders spoke differently, swore differently, dressed differently, and danced differently. They were called "Cherry Hoppers" the westsiders danced like the New Yorkers. We were dancing the Lindy hop and the Jitter bug or the slow Jazz. Another term used was Be Bop. Also, all the Italian names were spelled differently. (Mostly Sicilian on the eastside).

Our favorite place in the summer was Charlotte Beach with a famous Merry-go-round. There were four Life Guards at the beach. Spaces was not marked off, but you knew the dividing lines. Second life Guard was Westside only. You knew where to put your blankets .... believe me you knew! Third life guard was Eastsiders, and the first life guard was Jewish. The Charlotte kids were considered westsiders. We got along very well. At night, our hang out was the merry- go-round ... we never paid having learned how to jump on and off while it was running, always after the ticket taker collected we jumped on...and jumped off if we won the gold [It really was Brass] ring to show off, to a girl by presenting her the gold ring for a free ride.... We were "Big."

More of the Gang

1944-1948: High School

Here we go again, not Jefferson H. S. two blocks away but Aquinas was five miles away. Tuition was $75.00 per year plus $10.00 activities fees.

Jean was the sharpest Beast on the beach.
Jean, Mary and Mickey

My most memorable experiences were, while making a "Tower" we made four tiers shoulder upon shoulder. I was third Tier and "little Nick" was the fourth tier. Once, when we broke ranks I fell on a blanket with Two 10th Graders from Jefferson High .... I was a big time 12th Grader from Aquinas. I fell in the lap of my ever since sweet heart. She was the prettiest "Beast" on the Beach. (Beast was my personal term for the sharpest girls). Corny now! I was only fourteen years old.

Another memorable moment was when we the wise guys, were sitting and swearing and along came two sport heroes from the neighborhood. Vic Bonaldi played Football at St. Bonaventure and

Anthony Antonelli played in Ohio. They both heard us swearing and ripped us up and down. "You kids are a disgrace to our neighborhood, you swear because you cannot use the English language correctly." One thing was certain; we never used vulgar language if a girl or woman was anywhere near us. Al's stand was also a place of reverence. No swearing allowed by us, Al's wife Connie, daughter or sister in law might be present.

Chapter 2

1944-1948

Before graduating from grade school, I made my confirmation. My father's crony from the Avenue was my "Padina" sponsor. The age-old custom is for the sponsor to give a wrist watch to the boy or girl. My sponsor assured me that I was not to worry it was coming. To this day, I am still waiting. This created another Mantra for me. Anytime I am assured of something and told "not to worry" it will happen, I worry. IE: While playing 2nd base in the KPAA league I turned to our right fielder and told him to move back, I knew the batter from Aquinas. John gave me the signal not to worry about a thing. Tom Falk hit the ball at Kodak DPI field and it's still rolling. So, remember start worrying whenever someone tells you not to.

In the spring of 1944, Kodak came up with a great program. A softball fast pitch league was formed…. Any kids between the ages of twelve to sixteen could join as individuals or as a team.

Well, we were the Edgerton park gang and we played it all. Wow, they provided gloves, bats, balls and Umpires. Umpires were our heroes. These were all the ball players that played for Kodak Majors. Any one of them could have played Major League ball. But they made more money "working" and playing for one of the teams that Kodak had.

My friend Johnny Antonelli played for the Boston Braves and New York Giants and made about ten thousand dollars a year then and he was a Star in the Majors. We started with the thirteen years old. We were the Bisons the first year and won it all. The second year and for the next two years we were the Brooklyn

Dodgers....We won our League championship every year. Each member of our team was given a large panel for a wall indicating league champions.

Our KPAA Team our last year, ages 15 and 16.

The winner of each league championship got to play against the champions of other leagues. What a thrill. These games were played at Kodak Park under lights. The field was magnificent infield grass that was manicured, there were very few "bad bounces" if any.... I felt so fortunate, of a gang of at least sixty kids I owned 2nd base. For a skinny kid, I also owned the guard on our playground basketball team and center and linebacker on the football team. This is proud stuff, maybe even an ego builder. But this is the kind of stuff I needed. Acceptance is so important when you walk home alone from the "green grass." I would compete in my mind against the Japanese and the Germans; always with a ball in my hand. [*like what Greg does when working with Ashley in the yard.*]

MOVING ON TO HIGH SCHOOL

Same O, Same O, Jefferson H.S. three blocks from home and Aquinas was five miles away. But Aquinas had no one leave school for lunch policy. I was held captive for the day. Another thing about Aquinas, not all my friends could afford the $75.00 per year. When I arrived the only boys, I knew were the tenth and twelfth grade kids from Brown Square. So, not only the sisters and priests were my baby sitters, but also my older friends. OMG, I just figured that while at Aquinas, I knew some of the kids from Brown Square but in my three years I attended Aquinas, not one kid from the Green Grass or Edgerton Park was a schoolmate.

The great thing at that time was, Aquinas had Intra Mural sports like crazy. We had homeroom tackle football, basketball and no baseball. But I had all the baseball and football and basketball at building six. I did make the freshman basketball team, but then the imports and post-graduate students and scouted players were guaranteed a spot on all sports. We were forbidden to play against Rochester High Schools.

Aquinas achieved national headlines playing against schools such as Boys Town, Detroit Catholic Central and St. James of Texas. Some of these post graduates were twenty years old and even maybe twenty-two years old.

For some crazy reason, I became bossy. I was going to play that position and I was the boss. This was great in the ninth grade. Many of these kids went home that summer and hit some growth spurts and came back like giants compared to me.

Even the head coach was nationally known. Harry Wright was a tough dude win at any cost...he was my friend somehow, he thought I was a tough guy. This was far from the truth. I really had no choice because I was a little mouthy and felt it was us against the Irish and German kids. The sending schools such as Holy Rosary and Sacred Heart sent about twenty-five boys each to Aquinas. St. Anthony School sent three or four from, St. Lucy about three or four and one Eastside school called St. Francis sent three or four. Most of these kids were Italian. So, as it was more of us than them. But to this day I am still friends with all of them. And I must say that the Sullivan's, Clooney and all the Irish are still great friends of mine.

A lot of these kids I also knew from building six at Edgerton park. John Considine beat me out for the JV's Basketball. I was one of the last to get cut.... To this day, if I see John he is quick to tell me, "you should have made the JV's, you were better than me." I agree with him always. John J. Considine passed away today. God bless his soul.

I remember doing figure eights up and down the court for a layup. This is a piece of cake, right? Wrong, and I swear the last pass to me from the Irish kids, were always at my ankles. This may be sour grapes but, it is what it is. I remember going around the green grass one afternoon and telling George Delucia that I was pretty sure that "DA" and I made the JV's. "DA" was ten times the ball player I was. Domenic Anthony Viscardi picked Anthony for his confirmation name, because he wanted to be called DA.

Everyone had a nickname. My name in the bowling alleys was "Knarf Illerrob." Outside it was "Junior", named by another friend I would walk two blocks to his house for the last three years of grade school. His nick name was "Father Boff", his brothers were called Musty (because he loved mustard) and the other was "Bones" (because he was so skinny). These guys were from Jones Park and are great friends to this day. Dom and I both were the last to get cut from the team. Although no one had ever seen a one-handed shot. "DA" was the first person I ever saw shoot one handed. The original one-handed shot happened in about 1946. An Italian kid who was a star from Stanford University, his name was Hank Luisetti. He shot from the floor without the high jump shot, but like an old set shot with a bounce and like a set shot only one hand. "DA" later tried again in the eleventh grade and once again he was cut. In those days, the pro-teams averaged only seventy points a game. "DA" entered a Christmas tournament at the "Y" with a team from Brown Square. Most of the players were former college players and all over age twenty. Sunday morning, I woke up to read in the local newspaper "Viscardi breaks YMCA record one hundred and eighteen points in three games."

Now its January 1948 senior year, and Aquinas still cannot play local high schools. Father Carter the AD calls Domenic to his office and asks" Domenic where have you been these last three years." "DA" response was "I was here and you never knew I existed." "Well, you put on a uniform tonight we are playing Conesus freshmen" "DA" played ten minutes and scored twelve points. The coach went on the floor after the game and offered "DA" a full scholarship. He played four years and graduated, and then went on to become comptroller at the U of R.

Recently, I went to an Aquinas reunion. I was the only one there that graduated from Jefferson. I mentioned "DA" and his story and told all that would listen, that "DA" should have his name in lights at the school. I was told that a homeroom is dedicated to his memory. This was deserved, but the actual story was that "DA" endowed the school treasury with a large amount of scholarship money; hence the naming of a room for "DA." **C'est la vie.**

What is poor? Poor is having thirty-five cents for lunch and two bus tokens a day left on the kitchen table every morning. Bus tokens were worth a nickel. Each day we had a mission collection, some days two. It was Ra, Ra, beat one hundred and seven or Ra, Ra, beat two hundred and one and so on. All my lunch money was put into the collection. Some kids were "rich," they put in as much as twenty-five cents a day. They also owned a car. WOW, also maybe a boat on the river and a cottage on the lake in the summer. My tokens were resold for five cents to others for bus money.

Now, I had no or very little money left for lunch. What to do now? Two twin brothers must have figured it out. One worked the food line and the other was a cashier in the cafeteria. I would fake giving them money and every day for two years I had an egg salad sandwich and a carton of chocolate milk. I think God forgave us because we sent all our money to his poor people.... I tried to keep one token to take the bus home at least, if not I would have to walk home. I usually had an extra token ready for the second collection.

Even a few kids from Brown Square walked over a mile and a half to Edgerton Park. "Acey' Ristuccio and Sam Perticano would join me at the corner of Dewey Ave and Bloss St. This was at the end of the athletic fields of Jefferson High School. We would wait for the Hataway Bakery (Driver or Jockey). Keep in mind this was 1944 and the war was still going strong and there was a shortage of men and petrol. The driver was a woman and her truck was like a milk truck only it was a horse drawn milk delivery wagon used for bread delivery to houses. Patrons would display a diamond shaped card in their front window. Depending what point was at the top would indicate what was needed. The points were marked B for bread P for pies and maybe a C for cookies. This is about as good as I can remember, but it worked the same way. This driver began her route two blocks past Aquinas; "so who can ask for anything more." We also had a few cookies on the way. Imagine this day and age picking up three hitch hikers; I don't think so.

During this time, I also learned to forge the principal's signature WJ Duggan. A few of us would write an excuse from our parents to have us excused for various reasons. This was stupid, stupid and more stupid. What to do now that we were on the street? Winter or cold days we would go to the department stores and listen to records. Sibleys Inc. had about a dozen cubicles that were sound proof. Potential buyers would select a few and listen and then purchase one or more. Obviously, we had no money and would just return the records to the desk.

The best is when we would either go to a pool hall or a sport club. Both places were nothing more than a bookie joint. The pool hall occasionally we would get to see a Rochesterian, and none other than World Champion Irving Crane. He dressed in a tuxedo when he played for the Championships and he was World Champ more than once. We were there to mark the scores with a pool stick to slide rings [points] along a guide wire. Sport Clubs were different. These were outfitted with many tables for card players. There was a pool table with a removal top for a Crap Game if needed. This was usually after late at night. There were also some comfortable seats for those wanting to see the ball games on a wall. This is not TV here this is only a black board with innings and some info. lines for pitching changes or substitutes or delays. I still remember the "jargon" PPD rain, postponed for rain. We would get the information over Western Union Ticker tape. This was a glass enclosed roll of one-inch wide paper.

When it was printing something, it was the sound of a staccato ticking. These were also used in the stock market. All information was abbreviated. I remember a great guy who had a stutter, Patsy. If there was an unusual delay, that meant maybe the at bat team is having a good day. A favorite saying in the joint was not poking fun but laughing with Patsy. "Trouble in Cincy they were playing Washington. Pat had Tintanatti and Washington. And there was trouble in Tintanatti and he had bet on Washington."

If the weather was warm we would go swimming in the barge canal. Naked of course. I swam in that filthy water but it was warm. One day the police dragged the bottom with hooks to retrieve a body of an eighteen-year-old Sailor home on leave. That was the end of the Barge Canal for me. I could swim, but was never a good swimmer.

During this time, I was in the eleventh grade. I had a great job. At three O'clock I would go to a large stationary store Henirich Siebold and pick up my push cart. My job was to deliver stationary to all offices or hotels in the downtown area. On a rainy day, I had to deliver a package of stationary products to a Dr. Lindstrom. He was a graduate student from the U of R staying at a hotel on South Ave near Court Street. I went to deliver to his room on the second floor and the nicest, most beautiful woman answered the door. Hello…. Low and behold it was Ingrid Bergman, one of the most beautiful woman in the world. At that time, she was married to Dr. Lindstrom. Later while making a movie Stromboli she fell in love with the Director Roberto Rossellini. One of her other movies that was an all-time classic, was Casablanca. That was the good part of the day. The bad part of the day was that I got fired.

To complete the job by five pm was almost impossible. I had a large load and a few of the clients were not available. I returned to the store at five thirty pm. With one or two items not delivered, the store was closed, and it was pouring rain, I placed the cart in the alley behind the store. Really someone should have waited for me! But I lost the argument and was fired …I hated the job any way, I made more money setting pins.

Saturdays in the fall was for football. Our Edgerton Park team played Brown Square, Oak Street, La La Grande's team, Don Lamonica's team from # 30 school. We either played for Aquinas or Jefferson. The Russo brothers, Ange Ferraci, a top player for Aquinas in its day of the national ranking. We also played a Dutch town team and the Lyell Mt Read. So, one day we answer an ad in the local paper. "Irondequoit Bay Rats looking for a game on Saturday." This game was to be played at a church near Durand Park. We boarded a bus and paid our nickel. We passed the city limits and arrived in the Lake area of Summerville.

We arrived without equipment except for Billy Benedict. Billy had on a pair of bowling shoes. When we disembarked from the bus we were told that after the Zoo stop there is an extra charge of five cents. This was impossible to comprehend, so we all made a rush for the open door of the bus and started to run in all directions.

Omg, these guys had full uniforms, pads and matching helmets. When asked who we were in unison we hollered the "Edgerton Park Gang." They all swore at us and we were told to go home and get our older brothers. This was all said with a lot of profanity from both sides.

Now this was a challenge, it was us against a semi pro "wanna be." By gang tackling we could contain these Eastsiders. Last ten minutes or less the score was 0 to 0. Now we are 4th down and five on our own twenty-yard line. Punt, right? So, I hike the ball to Billy. A pretty good center direct to him. One step and kick, except his foot slipped and the ball travelled backward about ten yards. It was their ball, first and ten, on our ten-yard line. There was no way we could hold them and the final score was seven to zero.

This is who The Bay Rats thought they were playing.

This is who they actually played.

This was our crowning glory; a bunch of street kids beat up a semi Pro team. One exception, if we beat up on them, why are we hurting so. For the return trip home, we walked from Durand to the Seneca Park Zoo to board the bus. We all paid our nickel and slept well that night.

"Our Friendly Rivalry with The Brown Square Gang."
***Notice how many guys are in the Brown Square Gang*. Someone must have mentioned free food.**

As usual we were out numbered.
"We beat them anyway."

Old Timers Super Sunday

Edgerton Old Timers: [Front Row] Vince Messina, Nick Visco, Tony Marcella, Joe Nacca, Frank Borel

own Square Old Timers: [Seated] Ralph eroni, Blaze DiNardo, Lou Morganti, Lou Basso, Tantalo, Pat Formicola, Chester Palozzi, Cosmo rraro. [Standing] Anthony Maurizio, Dom chi, Ralph Antinonie, Frank Paris, Paul DiPonzio, Billy Ricci, Corky Baliva, Lou DiMarco, Dom Viscardi, Ralph Gentile, Jim White, Joe Dominick, Guy Bianchi, Pete Bianchi, Joe Visconte, Minni Palma, Tony Bianchi.

About eleven AM one school day I received a call from the principal's office. I was to get to the office ASAP. Now what? I am about 14 years old now. "Someone wishes to speak to me" When I arrive at the hall way near the front doors of the school, there is a large man standing there in the sunlight of the glass doors. He has a long nail file and is cleaning his nails. There is a taxi cab parked outside the doors. Can you imagine a fourteen-year-old kid watching an "old man" of about thirty-five years old filing his finger nails?

The total conversation went as follows." Hi, I'm Jim your mother's husband. Your mother would like to see you." My response was "she did not want to see me when I was a little kid, and I do not want to see her now." My memory of this is exact; I turned and returned to class.

Autres temps, autres moeurs

The Basilian Fathers that taught at Aquinas are originally from Canada. They are all a bunch of tough hockey players. Some of the teachers stepped over the line with punishment. If you were to get caught smoking in a bathroom Father Leahly might give you a healthy "whack." In the future, you went elsewhere to grab a smoke. The other teachers were Sisters of St. Joseph they were nice and I was totally familiar because they were the same order of those of St. Anthony.

Math and English were my two strong subjects; next came Latin. In fact, twenty years later I was teaching a class on Auto Insurance at Mercy High School and a little bitty nun came up to me in the cafeteria while pointing her finger at me. Shouting Borrelli, Borrelli, Francis you were in my Latin class. That's right Sister and I passed, right? Sister Concellia told me now and then, that I was a good student. She was one of the classes I never skipped. I mention this because I really could have been a good student with a little help. The kind of help I could have had at Jefferson High School. I also regret not taking this old Nun occasionally out for lunch. Never realized one can do such things. Years later a friend Ray Quercia mentioned that he met monthly with his grade school teacher from Holy Apostles School.

One afternoon after completing a final exam for Geometry, I placed my exam papers in the top left corner of my desk face down and remained in my seat waiting for the bell to end class. As was the custom. Father Bergeron wrote the evening homework on the front board. As I started to write the assignment, my pencil tip broke, sitting behind me was my cousin Sam Petracca. I asked Sam if I could borrow a pencil. I placed my hand on Sam's desk reaching for the pencil. *{There were no ball point pens in those days}.*

Picture this, my exam is in plain sight placed in the corner as is protocol. A small assignment pad is in front of me, and I begin to write the assignment. Suddenly I am struck over the head with a large heavy book, index finger still in book to keep his place. Father Bergeron was in the back of the room reading his daily prayers and he immediately became accuser, judge and jury.

I blacked out for an instant. When I felt a little clearer I tried to get up. I was wobbly and saw this "Midget Monster" hovering over me. I reached to grab his arm for help. Only me! The Cassock was torn at the shoulder and the whole sleeve was ripped off. I am dead! Get the hell out of here NOW! I ran out the front door and he ran out the other door. This is one of the few rooms with two doors. Room 201 usually used for a study hall and an exam room.

After two weeks, they managed to contact my father. Only twice have I seen my Dad angry. Keep in mind that his left hand was almost useless after that horrendous fireworks explosion. Lifting furniture for eight hours a day made his right arm and fist a lethal weapon. A few years earlier a wacko from the broom factory "Chico", was horsing around on his lunch hour. Chico grabbed me by my throat and put a choke hold on me. Fun, right?

Now, my Dad and I slept in the front room of our house. Dad was still in bed; he jumped out and was outside in five strides. Chico was about 6 ft. tall about 190 lbs. Dad grabbed his throat and decked him with a smash to his temple. OMG, he's dead! No not really, but he never sat outdoors or robbed our plum tree again.

Back to room 201, I left all my school things there and left school with no place to go. I think Aquinas got in touch with my Dad through the Parrish priest. OH, OH, another trip to the office, this time with my Dad. I was told to sit on the bench and be quiet. Dad proceeded to the desk to speak with Father Duggan, God, I remember this as if it were yesterday. Dad starts at the top of his voice; "where is that son of a bitch that hit my son over the head?" Father Duggan responds, "now Mr. Borrelli, no need to get excited." Dad now goes "berserk. Don't give me any of that shit, I want that no-good bastard down here so he can hit me in the head, I will pound him into that ground outside."

This tirade went on for a few more minutes finally Father Duggan convinced Dad that all will be OK and Francis will return to class. Great! Francis was returned to school but none of "the good ole boys" would teach him math. Francis accepted an "F" with a 90% average, this was true for a few other classes.

So off to summer school or night school, I forgot because there were so many. In night school, my final mark was a 98%. Did

I really need to copy from Cousin Sam? To this day, I wish that Father Bergeron had come down to the office that day.

Autres temps, autres moeurs

Today 2016 this would be a million-dollar lawsuit. As far as I am concerned Father Bergeron was and is, and to his death will be a disgrace to his "uniform." Certainly, this is not what God meant for these idiots to do in his name. This goof was a part of the basketball world at Aquinas, mostly Frosh and JV's. *Does this sound familiar David? Be sure to read the previous chapter about my dear friend Domenic Anthony Viscardi.*

Returning to Aquinas as a senior is not an option. My fellow classmates to this day treat me as one of the class of 1948. I am invited to all their luncheons and reunions. Some still remember that I was the only one that could ace Oral English every month by plagiarizing word for word our previous science instructor for two and a half minutes. Today, I cannot even remember what we had for breakfast this morning.

Jefferson H. S. here I come! Finally, my Dad gets the picture, to graduate I must change schools. I am still a 135 lb. fifteen-year-old skinny kid, able to fend for himself until five pm. I was to be a senior at this, the youngest in school history.

Most seniors need about three or four credits to graduate, I needed nine. The total number of credits to graduate in four years is sixteen. Mr. Swift decided I would not be able to complete the requirements, and placed me in an eleventh-grade home room 11/3.

Had I decided to remain in the 11th grade I would have hit a growth spurt of twenty-five pounds, and maybe an inch in height.

For some reason, I had "a hard head", Nonno Joe would call me "Capo Tosta." Nonno Joe was a live-in boarder; he was a good mason and worked at the trade until about age seventy-five. He was treated as a member of our family, and was a very good companion to my grandfather Borrelli. There is a strong possibility that he was married to my maternal Grandmother Maggie. Apparently, he split about the same day as my Dad separated, and both moved in with my Grandfather Borrelli.

The only way possible to take nine subjects was to take two in Summer school, one in night school and five during the day. This would give me eight subjects and if I took religious instruction one class a week at St Anthony's School, this would give me ½ credits. Choir was another option for ½ credits.... Total nine credits. Now I am on a mission. I pass the two in Summer school and now only need seven more remaining in normal school.

At the start of school, I sign up for five subjects English, Italian, Marketing, Modern Problems and one other. I pass the night school class and now have only the five classes left. Mr. Swift calls me down to the office to inform me that I might graduate, and I was put into Mrs. Pitoni's 12/3 home room. Not too bad. If I was to flunk even religion or choir I am dead. I skipped a lot of Choir, I could never carry a tune. I could do the "lu, lu,lu in the 'Battle Hymn of the Republic,' but that was it ,other times I would fake singing but no sound came out. Mr. Truit was about to flunk me and all would be for naught; fifteen and half would be close, but no brass ring. I pleaded with Mr. Truitt reminded him of how well I did as a cheerleader and in the Variety Show. Mr. Truit relented and gave me a "D+." I would now graduate with my class of 1948 at age sixteen.

Too bad now, I am still a skinny kid at 135 lbs. and five foot eight. After one year in the Army I was 158Lbs.and knew I could compete at any level. Most importantly all my friends my age and my girlfriend were two grades behind. Now, normal graduation age was eighteen years old.

Funny about the Army, if you are seventeen years old or fifty you are asked to perform any job needed for your designation.

DAY 1 OF SCHOOL TO JUNE GRADUATION

First day of school I went out for football. All the guys on the team were familiar to me. Our sand lot team played against most of these guys weekly. Every Saturday morning, we could be found at one of the neighborhood parks ready for a softball game or football game. Mr. Obrien the football coach took one look at me and said, "go home and be weaned, you're too small to play this game." I told him that I could compete with any of his guys." He told me to get lost!

Five years later Obrien was transferred to Franklin High School. The school had two gyms, at night the kids could pay a small amount and use one of the gyms. The other gym was used for the Rochester Industrial Basketball League. I was playing for Bausch and Lomb and had a game against Taylor Instrument at Franklin that night. In those days, we used that gym for our home games. This night, Mr. Obrien was sitting at a desk collecting coins from the students to use the girl's gym and clearing our team to the boy's gym. Mr. Obrien was now my buddy. We spoke briefly about the past and he admitted he should have given me a shot as a senior. Something weird also happened he asked about specific former girl student.

Next day in the Democrat and Chronicle there appeared a full-page article on "School Teacher Arrested," one super large scandal, involving Mr. Obrien and kids, boys and girls. Because of his age, he could move out of State to Ohio. Mr. Obrien left Rochester in shame. At that time, Public Schools had a National Honor Society for those students with a ninety average or better. My average was about seventy, but elected officers of the class would have an honorary membership. About the fifth day of school my girlfriend Jean, informed me that I was nominated to be a cheerleader, and tryouts were to be held that week. I told her to "get lost," because I was an athlete. Jean and her girlfriends worked me over and I was to believe to refuse would send the wrong message to the students.

Lisa, Joe, Mary, Mary Jane, Frank, Gloria, and Anthony ("PeeWee").

Joe Tese, Jean's brother was a cheerleader the previous year and his girlfriend Gloria, was the head cheerleader and would give me lessons before tryouts. The fact that Gloria was a "looker" helped also. I made the team. In front of the whole student body, I did the cheer on stage. It was a good thing I had no shame. "Boom Chick-a Boom" and so on, was this for real? My Mantra, again this was the negative, but the positive was that I was elected to the National Honor Society even if it was through the back door. Another positive was that while the football team travelled in old smelly bus, I was walking arm and arm with their girlfriends up Main St. to celebrate our victories.

Things were happening to our beloved Edgerton Park. First, they tore down our large Band Stand that stood in the middle of the park. Next came the Sports Arena. This was demolished, I grabbed two rows of seats. Too bad we were not Savers, in those days, these eventually ended up in the garbage. Our wonderful Museum of George Eastman's Trophy Room was made into a dry night club. This club was called the Stardust club. Entertainment for the club was provided by all the high schools in the area.

Joe Testa and Joe

Opening night entertainment was awarded to Jefferson High. As luck would have it a former student was on a visit to his home town of Rochester. None other than Mr. Pat Zicari, a top choreographer of the movie Industry. Mr. Zicari just finished the "Joelson Story" an award-winning movie about Al Joelson. Mr. Zicari committed to work with eight senior girls and teach them a chorus line routine.

"Show girls from Toledo"

The Stardust girls (five of the eight, I dated and one of the five is still married to me going onto sixty-five years. None other than Signora Jean) and Mr. Zicari selected a very appropriate Tony Bennet song called the Stardust serenade or Penthouse Serenade. "When were alone, just picture a penthouse way up in the sky with hinges on chimneys for stars to go by."

Our generation was born with work permits. While I still set bowling pins at night, word got out through the school that a machine shop on Water Street was hiring sixteen-year-old kids to work in the factory. I ran a kick press and a friend Joe Testa worked next to me. We put a metal nail into a slot and stepped on a lever this would activate a two-sided press and a belt buckle part was formed. Once formed a blast of air would send the buckle part into a large tray. Keep in mind, after placing the wire into the slot your finger had to be removed quickly. One-time Joe was talking to Lena Visco across the room. Joe left his finger a wee bit too long. When the blast of air ejected the part, along with it came a part of Joes finger. The tip was lying on the floor that was the end of the factory for me.

Next day, Joe Coccia and I went to Clapps Baby Food on Mt. Read Blvd. We both got a job dumping vegetables into a hopper that would clean and peel. After the cleaning, a conveyor belt would deliver these to a long line of women that checked and finished the cleaning the outer part of the veggies. These veggies came in sacks and the top of the sack had to be cut open with a long knife. I missed the top and cut a long gash on my hand. That was the end of that job. Joe decided to go to college and I would continue to set bowling pins till graduation.

Setting pins in a bowling hall was an art. Manual pin setting was much faster than the automation of today. I witnessed it evolve from manual to semi-automatics to automatics. We knew all the tricks of the trade. My cousin Frank Carsone was the bench mark of pin setters. He was so fast that the number one pin would still be spinning on the peg when he put the last of the ten pins into the pegs of the alley. A bowling alley is sixty feet from foul line to head pin. Immediately after the back row of the pins was a "Pit," about four-foot square and six inches deep. From the back wall, a large stuffed leather backstop was hung, this is what the ball would hit and drop in the pit. After the first ball was rolled all pins would be pushed to the left side or right side of the pit. I preferred the right side, so that my left foot could fit into the cut out in the front wall of the pit. Inside the cut out was a steel lever that if pushed down all the pegs would go up allowing you to set the pins on each peg. All bowling pins at that time had a half inch hole on the bottom.

I would grab four pins, two in each hand. First, I would set 1,3,6,10 then 2,4,5,9 and last the 7 and 8 pins, less if there was a miss by the bowler. I would set all ten in fewer than ten seconds. While a bowler rolled the ball, pin setters sat on one of the two walls that formed the sides of the pit, with legs straight out. If the pins "flew" up a little they would hit harmlessly on the backside of your legs.

A few things a pin setter knew with experience: 1. If there was a" soldier" left standing move the hell out of the pit. 2. If you did not like the person bowling and wanted to get even, on the first ball push the 8 pins between the 4 and 5 pins and the 9 pins between the 5 and 6 pins. This will almost guarantee a split. This cannot be detected from the foul line. 3. If the bowler rolls fast it's Ok to fake dying and lay next to the front wall of the pit. 4. If the person rolls a ball like Mrs. Demarco, very slow it's Ok to stay in the pit and catch the ball. The ball was removed from the pit and put on a sturdy rail for its journey back to the front rack. I had to use two hands for this. Nick Diponzio would lift the ball with one hand. Nick was also our fullback on the Edgerton Parkers. Great athlete!

Occasionally I "jumped alleys" and made $5.00 for the night instead of $2.50. Two alleys required you to sit on top of the side boards and swivel into the next alley. I wonder why I always fell asleep at last period in school.

A positive was that as a pin boy we would set for each other and just bowl all we wanted. All of us had a decent average, mine was about one hundred and eighty. My dad and I entered a Father and Son competition. We won with a combined total of twelve hundred and fifty scratch. Man, I was sweating till the last twosome finished at midnight. I kept telling my Dad over and over that "I really wanted this."

A great way to earn money was to set Back Row at Carbenau Bowling. The money bowlers developed this game for fast action. A bowler was given two chances for a strike or a spare as it is in regular bowling. The problem you were bowling against four pins. The sixty-four-dollar question was to go after a spare at two pins at a time, or go for a strike all four. If the pins did not fall from left to right as they rarely did you would end up with a big seven-ten split? Nice thing was after the contest all winners would throw at least $1.00 each to the pin setters.

Thrill of thrills; one afternoon, I set pins for Andy Varipapa, from Hempstead, L.I. Andy was the greatest trick bowler that ever lived. I think he was the greatest bowler that ever lived.

Now we come to the end of this cycle. I did what they said I could not do. Graduation night and there is a full auditorium. All graduates line up to have Mr. Swift hand out diplomas and give a word of encouragement. Ahead of me was John Antonelli. John was the top baseball prospect and a great guy. Swift told him good luck and it was great having him part of the school history. My turn, are you for real? Swift kept shanking my hand up and down. For what seemed like an eternity he kept telling me not to graduate and come back next year. Jeff was one of the only schools that had a GI Veterans school.

This Post-Graduate School had about 500 students; all were trying to complete their high school studies under the GI Bill. Mr. Swift promised that if I were to return I would be given a scholarship to any college of my choice. Yea, yea will you get lost? What a little jerk I was. Today I would call myself a young punk that was ungrateful. Mr. Swift and I remained friends for many years. This man was the greatest educator I ever met. This feeling I had although he would send me out to buy cigarettes while I was on a detention bench.

AFTER GRADUATION
1948-1950

After graduation, I got a job at Acme Optical Laboratories. Still only sixteen years old, I think I did a good job. The owner John and his wife Mary and an older kid about nineteen were his only employees. John was a brilliant inventor and designed many patents that were sold to Bausch and Lomb. We manufactured eye glass lens only. We also ground and cut lens to prescription requirements. On a rimless style, the lens was referred to as a P3 stock and we ground it to the script, concave or convex and if a bifocal is needed we attached the glass and ground it to specs. After we have the lens to the correct numbers we would drill two holes in the glass with a diamond drill. As we are drilling the hole precisely where the frame temple would attach we must constantly apply a cutting oil to lubricate and prevent the lens from cracking. I could produce quite a few of these daily. Unfortunately, one time a lens got too hot and the lens cracked in half. Oh, Oh I am dead!

While Mary was a great lady and kind, John was a little loud. John started to scream at me, this was a costly mistake on my part. After the tirade did not quiet down, I quit. What is there for me to do now sixteen years old? To enlist in the service, you must be seventeen with your parent's approval. We are still filled with a patriotism that will never be seen again. This did not take courage or guts, it's weird it seemed like such a no brainer. I knew nothing about the service or any other state or country. I saw a BB gun once that Sam Dauria had, we had no TV but most western movies showed some shooting. This was at least worth considering.

One day a friend Joe was going to look at the Marine recruiting requirements Joe and I graduated together and were classmates since first grade. I went with Joe to the recruiting office. All services have rules and regulations, for example if you were eighteen years. old, you would be allowed to join for one year. I would be seventeen upon my entering, at age seventeen you had to join for four years.

Hey, maybe, but let me get my feet wet first before I commit to such a long ordeal. Next door was an Army recruiting office, at age seventeen I could join for two years, but not get a choice of deployment or schools. Three years enlistment you could choose your place of deployment and school if you qualified. I was considering the Army for two years; I still am sixteen years old, the guys on the green grass got word that I copped out.

Unfortunately, Joe had feet problems and was discharged in a few months and my two years turned out to have added an extra year of fun and games in Korea. Where in the hell is Korea? A comment on the Marines, they did themselves proud in Korea. I served alongside many Armies from all United Nations. Marines, Brits and Turks earned my respect. Of course, GI Joe was pretty good also.

A few days prior to my seventeenth birthday I was on my way to ask the recruiter to come to my house. On the way, I cross two buddies from the green grass, Tata Messina and Nick Passerri, both were dear friends. Both Tata and the little "Midget Monster" Nick, were eighteen and had just quit school. Both were on their way to work, they threw their lunches in the air and said we are coming too. Both being eighteen selected Germany and we were separated after one week.

The big day arrived; September 07, 1948 my Birthday and D Day for the service. We met at the old Train Station on South Ave. This is now called Dinosaur BBQ. The only other person there was my Dad. Dad was a little emotional and I was a little scared.

Neighborhood Bars

Every neighborhood had a small bar where all men "hung out". These old timers would argue or bet on almost anything.

Games of Morra

"Morra" dates to the Roman times. This game can be played by two or by teams. The game is usually played for drinks. This can be a different thing of beauty. Let's say you are a team of five against another team. Only two played against each other at a time so, there are five games going on at once; game goes to ten. Each player will throw his hand out with one or five fingers showing. Let's say player one throws out three fingers and shouts "sette" (seven). The second player throws out four fingers and shouts "cinque" (five). There is no hesitation in the game as five calls may take only two seconds. In this case player, one has won a point.

There are many ways to win. That's a book in itself. But these are some of the ways that these friends spend their time. Not until I started to travel Europe did I realize what this was all about. All European countries have their local "hangouts." Italy has the contina, England and its Isles have pubs, Spain and Portugal has the La Barra. So, when our first generation arrived they were lonesome for their own familiar language.

The interesting part of this game is that after purchasing wine or beer, the winning team can approve or deny an individual of the losing team a drink. This of course, is done with plenty of theatrics. For example, the winning team selects a "boss"' and an "underboss," also called "padrone" and "sotte." The "sotte" invites a member of the losing team to have a drink; with this the 'Padrone' will refuse the individuals drink. This refusal comes out loud directly in the face of the loser, "Legitem!" they would say, in this case meaning no. After a while, individuals would take this gesture personally. As the loser's throat becomes dry, hostilities begin. This is the reason, in some parts of Italy for many years this game was forbidden.

Chapter 3

Upon arrival at Fort Dix I was assigned the first-floor bunk and Nick and Vinnie were on the second floor. At about ten pm a loud argument erupted upstairs. We all ran up and into the Barracks room. Little Nick is on top of his bed circling around like a boxer as if he was shadow boxing. Nick weighed about one-nineteen and he was arguing with this huge guy about two-twenty and six feet tall. The argument was about Jefferson HS having a better wrestling team than Franklin. Nick wrestled at one hundred and nine for Jeff and this brute wrestled unlimited weight for Franklin. The only thing that saved Nick was that he had forty guys on his side. Enough said, let's all go back to bed, tomorrow we start and Reveille will be at 0500 hrs.

Next few days was getting our clothes and physicals, with a little of exercise and orientation. {So far so good} My assignment was to ship out to Fort Devens. Mass. We will be there for eight weeks, or until we complete basic training with the 7th Calvary, 3rd Division.

A Division is made up of three regiments. This camp was formerly a woman's training camp during WW2. Now it was shared with this regiment and part of the University of Mass., in Fort Devens. Colleges were scampering for space after the war. The school utilized the old movie theatre and we could take courses for free.

After a few days, John Russo yells to me that he read in the Boston paper that a high school in Rochester went on strike. I located a copy of the newspaper; OMG! on the front page was a picture of Jean and all my friends from Jefferson high school. Coach Obrien tried to put the take on some of the money that John Antonelli made with the signing bonus. John was the first "Bonus Baby" in the major leagues. Obrien alleged that it was a promise made for all the special coaching that went on during John's High School. (Does this name seem familiar to the person collecting tickets at the gym next to where our factory basketball team was playing?) This picture showed Jean and many hundreds on the steps of building six. George Delucia and Jeans cousin Carl Tacci, the school President, were edging on the estimated crowd of one thousand. Jean was a cheerleader and led them in whatever had to be said. Boy, did I miss home.

The strike lasted only two days. Every newspaper in the country carried the story. I could just hear the other schools commenting on "those little" I -tal- ian" kids at Jefferson High School. "What do you expect".

TauTau and Nick shipped out to Germany after completing eight weeks of basic training at Fort Dix. After my basic training, we were all given IQ exams. The skinny kid, based on his exam scores was offered any school the Army had. I placed in the top five percent. Certain schools such as Officer Training School required you to sign up for more years. I selected Clerk Typist, MOS 3457. (MOS Military Operations Specialty) I still wanted to go to Germany but to do so would require me to sign up for a longer time.

There was two weeks left in Basic Training so I had to sweat out what next. Basic training was a lot of drilling, marching, confidence courses [formerly called obstacle courses] repelling cliffs of Vermont some KP. Ugh.... ugh.... I had to clean the grease trap a few times. Peeling potatoes was a snap, but cleaning up after three hundred hungry guys was no fun. Everyone had to do a part of that except if you had a few stripes I still am a lowly Private now.

One day, I looked out of a window and I saw a sailor walking with two of my friends, he asked them if they knew me. OMG, it was Dan "Butch" Marcone; my soul mate born on the same date and same hospital and lived almost across the street. Dan was our left guard on the Edgerton football team. Every time a big kid tried to hit me on the snap, rest assured Dan hit him hard. I think whenever we tried a quarter back sneak Dan and I made a wee bit of a hole for Sam Dauria our quarter back Dan was in a bar in Boston, his ship was in port. Dan lied about his age and enlisted at sixteen so, Seaman Dan was an old timer of about ten months in the Navy. We had a wonderful visit.

Six months later, Dan was caught and discharged. Dan was now eighteen so he joined the Paratroopers. Dan was one tough kid.

The following Monday I had to report to Fort Dix New Jersey for eight weeks of study. This was great duty. It was just as if we were in school. Classes were held from Monday to Friday then on Saturday and Sunday we visited all the towns in Mass. Boston was quite expensive, our favorite was Worcester Mass. These people were so patriotic we were treated fantastically well.

My average was over ninety percent and my typing was at least forty-five words per minute. The test for typing was given with all keys painted black. Word was that all kids that failed went to Germany. One thing about the Army there never is a lack of rumors. So, smart ass Frank and another jerk Joe Bucci decide we will fail and go to Germany. This was the most disgraceful thing I have ever done. I humiliated myself and on my discharge at least they wrote school "clerical awarded MOS none" Joe got cold feet at the end and decided to pass the re-test. Joe passed and I failed. That day my orders were changed unknown to me. These orders were given instead to Joe Bucci from Brooklyn. I would never see Joe again. The original orders were to me. To: Private Frank Borrelli Jr. RA 1211 report to dock NYC at 0800 tomorrow for duty on the USS Mercy Hospital Ship; this ship will travel between Bremerhaven Germany and NYC.

Not only did I disgrace myself, it makes me sick to think of what I threw away. A reputation that was worth a million dollars suddenly was worthless. A vow was made to God and me that day that I would be the best that I can be from that day forward. Six months in the service and I was only a lowly private. I was an overachiever and not an under achiever. I proved that with the exhibition in the 12th grade with nine subjects to graduate and I did it. Now only seventeen and one hundred and thirty pounds and I am making promises to God and me not knowing what is in store for me. While waiting for my orders I got a Christmas leave. Went to the PX and the last showcase on the right contained a small cross and chain with several cut diamonds. There were no credit cards in those days and I paid a half months pay for $40.00 for the chain and cross. Jean has worn that cross almost every day for sixty-five years. What to do with Private Borrelli while waiting for orders? I was put in charge of all furnaces for eight different barracks. These stoves were in a separate room at floor level. I quickly learned you could delay the need for more coal by "banking" the fire. So, I banked the fires and went to sleep for one hour. Eight hours later the lieutenant came into the barracks and threw me out of bed. All fires were out and all barracks were freezing. So far, I am nothing but a "Sad Sack GI." I am not getting off to a good start in "this man's army."

After a couple of weeks my orders came through. Report to the Infantry School at Fort Benning Ga. 30th Infantry Regiment, Third Infantry Division. It is what it is! I will make the best of it. This fantastic blunder was made by a juvenile delinquent. It will not be the last but thanks to you God we had more good calls than not.

Fort Benning was the home of the 82nd Airborne also known as the All-American Division. These are one bunch of cocky proud soldiers. This outfit was the best of the best. These guys set the bar so high that only a few would measure up. They believed in what they were told by those that came before them. Their record in WW2 was something that they were proud of. We all got along well occasionally some idiot would step on a trooper's boots looking for trouble, and they got just that. On my first day, I met a guy from Fall River Mass. His name was Adolino Flores. From day one we were the best of friends. Al was Portuguese and had a lot of the same values as Italians. From that day on, we were together to our last day sharing a small hole thinking we both were ten days' overdue for our "trip home." "There are no atheists in a fox hole" this is an axiom. That night our position was hit hard and we had to withdraw to a lower position, until we had some additional support from the Turks. We prayed together that night and we made it home safe.

Our first night in town, wow! The south and the Army were segregated now. Columbus is separated from the nearest town by the Chattahoochee River. This town is Phoenix City Ala. the toughest town in the USA. Of course, we had to visit Phoenix City. As soon as we arrived in town by bus, we noticed a large crowd on the river bank. We went close to the police barricade and found that a corpse was found at the river's edge he was murdered. The gentleman that was murdered was called "Blue Jay." The body was found in Alabama but, the trail of blood started on the Georgia part of the bridge. Having found this out the Phoenix police now wanted no part of the operation. Leave the body until the police from Georgia arrive. I found this to be a little strange way of doing things. Once again, a different time, and a different place.

Fort Benning was made up of two major areas the Main Post and Sand Hill. The Main Post housed the 82nd airborne training facilities. Also, based on the main post was the 15th Infantry, Regiment 3rd Infantry Division. The 3rd Infantry Division at that time was made of the 7th Cavalry, the $15^{th,\ and}$ the 30th Regiments. My new friends and some old ones made up a part of G Company Thirty Infantry Regiment. A company consists of three rifle platoons and a weapons platoon. Based on my test marks I was placed in the top percentage and was put in the weapons platoon. Shown once, I could take the firing breach of a 57MM recoilless rifle apart blind folded and re-assemble it back blind folded. This weapon was 4ft. long and 45 lbs. I was now ranked Cpl. {two stripes}. We still had to qualify in all small arms. We qualified on a 45caliber pistol, Ml Rifle, and Carbine thirty caliber. As was the Ml a BAR Automatic, both were air cooled and water cooled 30 caliber machine guns.

We learned how to use rifles and hand grenades. This grenade tossing was a trip; I always hoped I threw far enough. Mostly we threw into a sand bagged enclosure. We also had to qualify on the 3.5 bazooka, and we learned how to field strip these weapons and then re-assemble them. Cleaning could be tricky, my pistol I carried had a wee bit of Cosmoline, a packing grease in the firing mechanism. I removed all the inserts that were inside the grip, this consisted of two main springs loaded to control the firing pin. For eight hours, I worked on trying to replace this spring bar to no avail. Had I not fixed it "I would have to pay for it." I really don't think I would have to pay but I fixed it in time for inspection next day.

My platoon had three squads of mortars and three squads of fifty-seven recoilless. My squad consisted of myself as a gunner and my assistant gunner that loaded the shell through the breach, then tapped my helmet when in and locked. Our squad also had seven ammo bearers. These shells were color coded for armor piercing, anti-personnel and white Phosphorus. I thought I was pretty good at this and my "old" platoon Sgt. liked me.

Everything we did was competitive, squad against squad, platoon against platoon, and Company against Company and so on. Funny, I thought I was pretty good with a pistol. Upon being discharged I was trap shooting with my brother in law Joe and friend Joe Nardone. After, we started to shoot pistols. It's a good thing that we were not betting or they would have cleaned my clock.

One day we were told that President Truman was coming to inspect the Camp. He was our commander in chief. Our company was selected to perform a "mad minute" for him and staff. This is a situation where a large part of the company making sure there is at least one of each item in our arsenal to be used. I was selected to be at the end of the firing line with my 57MM Recoilless. All live ammunition is to be used. We were told on the loud speakers that anyone turning to the grandstand with a weapon would be shot on sight. The previous evening before sunset I took my 57MM to an open field. I removed the firing pin from the breach. At the front opening of the weapon there were four slots cut in at 12 o'clock 3,6 and 9. With a rubber band I made an X. The center of the X is in perfect line with the hole left where the firing pin was. Next, I sighted on a pole up on a hill about fifteen hundred yards away. Next, I sighted through the telescopic lens and saw the same pole, in both cases I used the left side of the pole to get the sighting as close as possible. Now, when I aim at the picture, I see is exactly where my shell should hit. My piece is ready to go now. This is called Bore Sighting. Your aim is what you see you will hit.

Bore sighting the night before the President's visit.

This was one of the duties that were part of the tough side of the nineteen months. Hey, let's face if in those days someone mentioned that you would see the President of the United States the next day you would be a basket case. This was George Washington, Abe and all past Presidents rolled into one. What an honor for the skinny kid from the Green Grass.

At about seven am we lined up in a straight line facing a ravine. Fort Benning was large enough to have firing ranges to accommodate just about any firing of live ammunition. My position was at the extreme right end of the line. President Truman was directly behind me, about thirty yards away. Keep in mind that, this is live ammunition we are using here. An announcement is made that if anyone faces the grandstand with a weapon in hand, that person will be shot on sight. So much for all that.

There is enough fire power here to wipe out a small town. We will be firing from one hundred yards to fifteen yards at mockup of Infantry and some old armored tanks and troop carriers.

The command was given "ready on the left, ready on the right, commence firing." Now, all hell broke loose. With the help of my assistance gunner, I could get four rounds off and to the targets. Not too bad, I hit both tanks, and dropped two shells into the middle of the infantrymen."

President Truman called our commanding officer; keep in mind that Mr. Truman was in the artillery in WW I and our 57 MM recoilless is the closest thing to an artillery piece. "That was some mighty fine shooting from that young man." That's me the skinny kid from Montrose St., man, was I proud.

Gliders were a fascinating aircraft. These were used by Airborne Infantry during WW2. On the invasion of Normandy, the Germans in preparation for the carriers landing troops cleared a large farm area so they could land a couple thousand 82nd Airborne. "You think"? Wrong they cleared a forest to appear like a meadow. One exception was that there were hundreds of tree trunks camouflaged to look like nice grass. Unfortunately, our miscalculation cost us two thousand casualties.

We were given a familiarization in case ever our infantry could be deployed in such a manner. First, we learned to load all our equipment and how to depart using a PLF (parachute landing fall), "bend knees to left and put weight on the right side, next to buckle up in the seats." Picture this, two poles about fifty feet apart a rope line connecting at top of poles. Our glider tethered to this line and a DC3 Aircraft trailing a heavy wire with hook flying over at about one hundred feet above and scooping up your line. It is a sudden jolt and then you are "up, up and away" you are released at about a thousand feet for a free landing back to a landing field. **Autres temps, autres moeurs.** This was a short-lived experiment and no longer are gliders used since 1949 or 1950.

The "chicken shit" part was inspections and cleaning details. Barracks inspection was conducted every Saturday morning. If you or the Barracks failed inspection there would be no week end passes. This left us no alternative but to have a coke party on Friday night.

A Friday night a coke cola party consisted of all of us, about fifty of us armed with vintage coke bottles. These bottles had the embossed lettering on the bottles. Asses and elbows is all that you can see. We would get on our knees and form ranks of five across each line would follow the previous line. On our knees, we would scrub the floors with the bottle, this would give the floor a burnished look. These darker spots would almost shine. When we arrived at the end of the room we proceeded to the beginning, other ranks followed. This operation was done as many times required to achieve a complete covering. Also, you better be sure your "piece" rifle, carbine or pistol was free of any dirt even a spec. Foot locker had to be opened and all items lined up like a bunch of soldiers.

Shoes had to be spit shined to a high gloss with shoe strings perfectly spaced. I paid Rocky twenty-five cents to lace my boots. All items of clothing had to be hung with the shoulder patch lined up even. Sometimes we pinned the shirts and jackets in line to achieve maximum alignment.

Competition in Physical Education was every month. I hated pushups and pull ups, but could achieve the min. requirement. This has never happened to me before or after. While doing the squat jumps I achieved a weird "euphoria" and went on a roll. I could almost go on indefinitely but I did get to over two hundred seventy and stopped. This beat out the two hundred men in our company, I won a three-day pass, starting on Thursday night to return on Monday for reveille. This was my 4th 3-day pass. At 4:30 on Thursday I took the free Army bus to town, Columbus Ga; and started to hitch hike home. All alone I would start at the main high way towards Atlanta. I had a dress uniform on and looked like a real soldier. In those days people would pick you up, especially the trailer truck drivers.

Apparently, these guys needed some conversation to stay awake. The worst was once at the bridge in Harrisburg Pa. I was offered a ride on a Harley Davidson motor cycle to Lima, New York. I was dropped off at the four corners in Lima and fell flat on my face. My legs were numbing from just hanging on the sides; there were no buddy seats on this thing; total elapsed time to get home was twenty-four hours. I arrived in Rochester at four pm. We must not forget Earl Cohen. He lived off Monroe Ave. we became good friends, although he and I were miles apart. Earl once started a fight in Phoenix City and caused the whole place to erupt. He was a little under the influence and stepped on a Paratroopers shoes. Then he slides under a table and watches the festivities, complaining a girl was going to kill him.

One weekend he decides to come home with me. We start hitching at about five pm; about two in the morning we decide we would have one sleep for thirty minutes and the other hitching. This lasted one trick, my turn to sleep I put him on guard duty. My buddy falls asleep on duty. After about ten minutes a car comes by about sixty mph, the wind from the car rolled the two of us into a ditch by the side of the road. We were asleep about two feet from the road, not too smart.

The car stops, and some drunk got out of the car, he thinks he ran us over, he is thinking he killed us. He is so happy we are alive that he picks us up. The plan is for him to take us about twenty miles. After ten minutes, he asks if we have a license to drive. Earl did have a license to drive and agreed to drive the next twenty miles and the man was to sleep in the rear and try to sleep it off. After two hundred miles, the man wakes up and goes insane. After a little profanity, the car owner leaves. In his condition, he had no choice. **"Autres temps, autres moeurs."**

I arrived home at five pm. With no sleep for twenty-four hours. I showered and shaved and off to see Jean, and dinner with friends. We arrived at Doris Magrissi's house and met her beau later to be husband George. Also, there was Mickey Salerno and boyfriend Alex Riola also to be husband. The six of us waited at the house for a bus; conveniently there was a stop in front of her house on Jay Street.

The six of us lined up at the corner I was leaning on the pole while the five got on the bus. As the bus departed, I was still asleep standing up leaning on the bus pole. Fortunately, after a block I was missed and George came back for me.

The best was while walking to the pier I spotted three "lookers" from the east side on a blanket by the third life guard. I left my companions and asked if I could sit with these Beauties. This was Ok because I had received a Dear John letter from my friend Jean. This was June 1949 and I had expected to be discharged in fourteen months….

The next week back at camp I received a "Dear John" letter. I think the folklore is "Dear John I sent your saddle home." Jean was entering her senior year in high school and became infatuated with a drummer and good dancer. Tom lived next to my young cousin Phillip Carsone. Apparently, Phillip was "Gung Ho" military. His brother was a POW in WW2. Phillip later became a Paratrooper. His mail was always the same, asking me when I was coming home so he can help me kill Tom. The truth is, twenty years later we built a new home and Tom and his Dad did all the electrical work.

I wanted to get home and the only way was to go AWOL (absent without leave). My plans were made, get to Atlanta and buy a one-way ticket to New York. My friend Rocco from East Harlem decided to go with me. Off we went; we are boarding the bus Rocco is already on and I started to board. Suddenly two big MP's grab me and ask to see my pass. I am on a week end pass, and it is ten o 'clock on Friday. The MP's looked at my one-way ticket to New York and knew I was not going to make roll call on Monday from NY. "Come with us young man you are under arrest."

Into Fort Mc Phereson I am going in a squad car. The duty officer starts with the questions. My case is that it is Friday and I have until Monday to get to base; so, I am not AWOL yet. After an hour, he gave me a direct order "to go immediately back to base." This is exactly what I did and said**" Cei Ie vie."** I never made it home to see Jean. So, now I begin my sabbatical from spring of 1949 to the summer of 1952.

Months later I went to Harlem to look up Rocco. What an experience, no one knew him or at least was willing to talk to me about an AWOL soldier. When I returned, I took Rocky's shoe polish brush and keep it for safe keeping. I still have Rocky's brush at home for safe keeping. Three months after the fiasco, I was on guard duty and assigned to prison detail. Here we would line up and get a squad of eight or less and walk with them while they did outside chores, like sweeping streets, painting and cutting grass. There was Rocco in line we said hello but I had to decline. Before any of us could do this, we had to view past incidents where the prisoner chaser was too friendly and was removed of his weapon and killed. Obviously, I did not want to be friends with anyone.

Things were back to normal now and I could see more of the opposite sex in Columbus. As luck would have it, I was pretty good at making out in the movie theatres. We had so many movie houses in Rochester so experience was easily gained.

I offered an attractive young eighteen-year-old southern gal a coke. She spoke so nice except I had to pull the words from her mouth. Martha and I were “a thing” for about six months. One cannot wonder what happens to old friends. I was best man at a wedding for Stan Rose my closest friend in Korea; It has been thirty years that I have been trying to find out what happened to Stan and his wife Angie. That was a happening Stan, Jewish and Angie Gagliano an Italian. Angie's brother Marty was a runner up for Mr. Universe. He had deep cuts in his stomach; I thought it must have been a big operation. Hello, these were called abs?

In September 1949, the South and Armed Forces were desegregated. I seemed to have a lot more in common with the blacks than the others. I enjoyed their music and sort of laughter with each other. I had a harder time getting close to the puerto ricans. Language was not my strong point, but a few words in Italian were similar and the religion. The blacks taught us how to do a shuffle step and incorporate it into our marching. This was done when the drill Sargent was not looking. Of course, on each beat was a swear word, also incorporated into the march.

In our travels around the post, we visited the football field. Fort Benning had a great football team. I am not sure what teams they would play against, but I would guess about a Division III level. Both Dan and I agreed that we could compete with these guys. Dan transferred to Fort Bragg and actual played for their team. He was scouted by The University of North Carolina State. Dan quit school in the tenth grade, and they gave him a certificate of completion a GED and gave him a full scholarship.

Norma

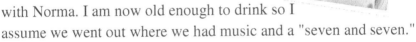

Christmas 1949 was a great time; both Dan and I were home. We played eastsiders and hung with Norma and friends. Snacky started dating Lena, later broke up and Carl Nacca married her. No relation between Snacky and Carl. Vito still was dating Jo, and I was with Norma. I am now old enough to drink so I assume we went out where we had music and a "seven and seven." Seagram's 7 and 7Up, was the drink of the teen drinkers. Borrelli the match maker **"matchmaker, matchmaker make me a match."**

Christmas Time 1949

After the first of the year it was back to Fort Benning to continue training for our amphibious landing onto Puerto Rico. That winter training was in Little Creek Virginia. While training my Platoon Sargent, he was one of the first men down the ladder, sad, I forgot his name but he saw a lot of action in WW2, and was trying for his twenty years. He must have been in his fifties. His hands slipped from the sides of the rope, as he was falling a high wave struck the landing craft and raised it about ten feet up and into the ship. He was killed, this was my first sight of a casualty. God Bless him he was a good man. Sadly, I do not remember his name.

Finally assault on Vieques, fun and games it was, us against the Green Army. Different troops from a different organization are dressed in a uniform with green trim and modified clothes to appear very German looking.

Now for rest, we were given a three-day pass and I met Olga Dinez, the singer at the Caribe Hilton. The Hilton was and still is the best hotel and night club in San Juan. We visited Morrow Castle and just had a nice time.

I just turned eighteen and met a gal, she was about twenty-one. I still remember the address Bornio Ampano, stop thirty-six. The song she sang was Caminando, Caminando etc. Nice family and they welcomed me as a friend. The summer of 1950 I had a two-week furlough home prior to the anticipated discharge in September.

On about the 26th of June I received a Telegram from Fort Benning to return to base immediately, the North Korean Army has invaded South Korea. Where the hell is Korea?

After fast good-byes, I returned to Base. When I arrived, I found it was like a ghost town. Before leaving town for home, I borrowed $10.00 from Romano. Russo and all friends that had more than one year left on their enlistment were put on a plane and shipped out to the assembly area in California.

All these guys were sent to **the lst Calvary, 2nd Infantry Division, 24th Infantry Division and** various combat positions. They were needed to replace many casualties that our divisions were losing. Our first responders were outnumbered ten to one. Generals were taken prisoner many more casualties that decimated their divisions. All that was left of South Korea was called the Puson Perimeter. This was almost ten miles from being thrown into the Sea of Japan. If help did not arrive it would be all over.

Picture a line drawn on a curve from coast to coast with Puson at the edge. Fortunately, these troops from every camp in the USA were arriving hourly. While in town one day, I saw a news display in a store window. "Paul Romano" heating his coffee on a fire" OMG! That's the guy from St. Marie that I owe $10.00 to.

Now what do we do at base? My squad of twelve was cut to three, and of the ten-thousand soldiers in our division we had about three thousand. President Truman makes a great decision. All members of the Armed forces with less than one year left on their enlistment are given one more year. Because of this law I now have fourteen more months to go before discharge. As the Marines say **'Semper Fi. '**

About this time, General Mac-Arthur was planning an end-run landing at Inchon. When our commanding General was asked by Mac-Arthur if our Division was up to it, the response was "yes Sir." We were at thirty percent of our minimum requirement. Of the ninety members in our platoon we had less than thirty. We had no ammo carriers or other skilled operators of this equipment. Yet here we go. Bag and baggage all equipment is expendable go to the supply room and get any new clothes needed. We were given a basic list of what should be in our duffle bag. I sent everything I had home and got all new stuff. New is not always better. My clothes were soft after so much washing; new stuff was stiff as a board.

While on board our troop ship, I saw that sailors tied their fatigues to a rope and threw the rope over board and the salt water would almost bleach the material and after one washing to get the salt out they were soft. I tried this knowing that I never could tie a good knot. A brand-new pair of fatigues were tied to a line and thrown overboard. The wake of the ship was pouring out a three-foot-high twenty miles an hour wake. Not even ten minutes and my new pants were sailing to meet Davy Jones Locker.

A troop train was waiting for us at the station in Columbus. This was a Pullman one upper and one bottom. Your two seats opposite were very roomy and made into a bunk beds. This was very comfortable for our two-day ride to our Port of Debarkation, Vallejo, California. We stopped the train in KC, KS. We all disembarked and marched to the center of town. The town had a park in the center of their main area. We proceeded to do calisthenics for about an hour and then back on the train to finish our eight-day trip.

We are trained but do not have a clue what is going on. Apparently, MacArthur found out how bad we were decimated with the loss of our men and hit the ceiling. We stopped in Hawaii, but docked three miles out. We had to resupply because now we were going to Japan to train our new recruits, whatever that means. As we progressed we passed the International Date Line on September 7, my birthday now that date goes from the 6th to the 8th. My birthday was never seen by me, does that mean I am one year younger? Oh Well!

After five days, we arrived on the Southern Island of Japan Kyushu, this is where in the city of Beppu they have the mineral baths, OMG they are the best in the world and off limits to all of us.

We were placed on top of a mountain and put up large squad tents and medical facilities. The next week hundreds of young Korean men arrived with their civilian clothes on. These men were just swiped off the streets and told they were in the Army. We supplied them with all uniforms, helmets, mess-gear and toilet articles. Immediately they had a ball, they have no or very little facial hair and were given a safety razor. I could not believe my eyes they started to shave first their forehead and then nose and cheeks. OH, OH, we should train these people? What we did not know was that the Korean men and women are very intelligent. The Korean Country was occupied by Japan for many years, and never given a chance to prove their worth. I loved these little guys with the similar names. Somehow it seemed all had Kim in their names IE Sang Su Kim, this was my man. He came to us with a shirt and tie and was my number one assistant gunner.

These little guys came to us from a whole different culture. Personal hygiene was non-existent. It was funny, but they were intelligent and great guys. I really got close to some of them, I knew they had my back.

As was the custom our tent held about forty men; plus, all our clothing, ammo and other supplies. Ammo was carried in a two-sided jacket, vest in front and back pack in rear total of eight rounds split four and four. These were stored in a corner of the tent. There were no lights or heat in the tent. Not to worry, American ingenuity will prevail. A helmet was put on the floor and filled with gasoline; this being lit became a great source of light. After a few minutes, someone tripped on the helmet and a gallon of burning gasoline covered all the ammo.

A bucket brigade was formed within a few seconds. The ammo packs were thrown from man to man until the guy outside placed them away from the tent. One of the last ones I caught had a cupful of burning gasoline in a pocket. I caught all the ammo and a cup full of fire. I was a human torch and Sargent Spears was removing his jacket as you would a sweater over his head. This was the fastest way for him to get it off and help me snuff out the fire. I was blinded by the flames and could not see straight, to me it looked like Spears was standing with his arms folded watching me burn. "Spears you son of a bitch give me a hand in putting this fire out." By then he came with his field jacket and helped me put out the fire. We hugged and now I knew what was meant by having someone guard your back. We had some fun and games and shared some laughs and tears for the next year.

Medics transported me to a field hospital. I did not want Morphine for fear I would be an addict. So, I remained in pain, the guy in the next bunk gave me a bottle of 3.5 Army Beer and that put me to sleep. After five days, I was returned to my outfit. I would spend all days reading and thinking. My gunner was promoted to Squad leader in my absence. This was great, on a firing line the 57mm is up front in case there is an attack or maybe a tank supporting the enemy advance. Now the mortars are a "safe" thirty to forty feet behind the line. You have no idea how much safer this is. Sargent Jarrell had a mortar squad without a squad leader and gunner. This mortar was left back at camp all day. Within a week sitting on my fanny or my belly (My right leg was an open book and I had to keep it bandaged from my ankle to my thigh). I could get a mortar from a stored position to a firing position and levelled at sixty degrees' elevation and 0 to center. And ready to fire signal or shout. I was told by Sammy Jarrell that the record for this was twenty seconds to get the first round on the way. I was at about twenty-five seconds and asked Sammy to let me transfer to his mortar section. I kept practicing between my visits to the hot baths every day. The burns would not heal and it was felt the Sulfur baths would help.

Company gets order to ship out to Korea and disembark in Pusan to help support the Pusan Perimeter. Cpl. Borrelli will remain behind and by hospital train, proceed to Nagoya Army Hospital. This train had about thirty beds, bunk style in each car. We passed through the outskirts of the city of Nagasaki the second Atom Bomb site. Wow nothing but a few twigs were left standing, miles and miles of torched land. Today it is one of the most magnificent cities in the world.

I was on the top bunk and other ambulatory wounded were coming on board. A handsome six-footer had new army fatigues on and a hat with one side up. The US furnished all our fellow United Nation allies clothing and supplies. "Where in the hell did you get that hat?" I said. Hello, he was from Australia. He wanted to smash me; I showed him my bandaged leg and he backed off. That Campaign hat is worn proudly especially if you have earned the right to fold up the right side showing you are a combat veteran.

Yayeko Matsomoto
Her Dad liked me.

Nagoya Station Hospital was a great place to get three more weeks of rest. I became the champion fly killer. I used a trusty rubber band and walked the floors for an hour a day. And walked to town one day; I met Yayeko Matsomoto, I think she was the prettiest Japanese girl I had ever seen. I met the Mama San and Papa San.

(Jo san was eager to introduce her hero to her family). We had a nice visit, my division patch told them that I was back from Korea. Ok, so I played the hero, how would I ever explain in Japanese. It was only a few days later that I did rejoin my outfit in Korea.

After a few weeks in the hospital some of us ambulatory patients were taken on a little R & R to the former Hirohito's Imperial Palace Estate. He was seldom seen unless he was on one of his white stallions, either White Snow; Sirayyurki or First Frost; Matsimo Shimo. I was put on one of these gorgeous animals. This animal knew I was a rookie. He kept turning to the left to bite me. Another thing, he kept running along the fence to scrape me off. Finally, I let go of the reins and he proceeded back to the barn. I have not tried to ride a horse since.

Korea: War is Hell

Beautiful Horse,
White Snow; Sirayyurki

It is not my intention to tell war stories. Most of us that walked the walk do not wish to talk the talk. Someone once said, "War is Hell."

This is true and I would like to add the following. But, War also produces leaders, and provides education. College will give you four credits for Military Science. Sometimes you can experience humor, sadness and gladness. You can gain closeness to your God. You can gain new friends, some of which will remain lifelong friends. I experienced love, hate, confidence and new swear words. I believe the most positive happening was that I gained an ability to understand different cultures and ethnicities.

Very little impresses me especially wealth or status. Give me intelligence and attitudes such as honesty, giving and caring. I judge people solely one on one. The Army changed the name of the obstacle course to Confidence Course. I truly have gained confidence in my abilities to lead and learn.

Life marches on, I now am promoted to Sargent. Not bad for a nineteen-old skinny kid from the Green Grass. Now the draft is bringing a lot of experience to Korea. Many ex-combat infantries from the European theatre of war and the Pacific are arriving daily. Wow, today Melvin Gooley has arrived, Mel is a three-year veteran of the war in Europe. He is an expert gunner on a 60-mm mortar.

The next day Corporal Lecouver arrived. I asked him to do something and he refused. "I am a full Colonel and am here on General MacArthur's request." (Permanent rank is what you arrive into combat with all future ranks are temporary until you leave the war zone). IE my permanent rank is Corporal and I achieved Sargent.

Always had a "cig" going. Notice the bracelet.

First class the second highest noncommissioned officer rank there is. So, Corporal Lecouver why are you a Colonel? "I oversaw all the Filipino Guerrillas and the General made me a Colonel. "And you are an Ethiopian loving bastard, I am going to knock you on your ass." "Stanley where is Ethiopia?" Stan Rosenstein (Rose) was my friend. Stan was Golden Gloves NYC Champ and European champion at welter weight. He told the Corporal " First you fight me, then you fight my Sargent." That was it for the story, next day he was gone. Mac Arthur sent for him, I have read since that the General loved cronyism. But the story on my dear friend Stan reads like an exciting novel. "Stan was a former Trust Trooper." These were the occupation troops stationed in Trieste.

This Regiment was by far the "sharpest of the sharp." Army combat boots are smooth side in and rough or suede side out; this is in case the GI had to go barefooted without socks. They would take the boots to a shoemaker and have the cobbler turn the boot inside out and rebuild the boot. This effort was necessary if you want the best shine one can get. Now I think they have fake leather called "cordovan "on their dress shoes.

The 15th Infantry Regiment was deployed along what was called the Pusan Perimeter.

The stakes are about ten inches apart.

This whole war was a go North then retreat south, then back up North, now back down South. I am out of the 57-mm rifle section and I am a mortar gunner. To traverse left or right or shorter or longer you must have a center state to aim at and others to the left and right. Stakes are about ten inches apart. Each stake would represent about twenty yards.

Someone needed as a forward observer to establish contact with my radio man. My man would convey messages IE in yards "up ten, right twenty etc. ten yards would be one click on the tube up. Twenty yards to the right, maybe two click to the right. This was accomplished with the aid of a leveling sight with a regular level bubble in the scope. Unlike a rifle scope where you see the target these shells travel out of sight maybe a thousand yards or so. There are three types of ammunition, high explosion, White Phosphorus and Illumination. Most of the enemy, as was the case of our GI's, always dug into our positions. Being a few inches below the height of the ground was prevention for incoming rounds of artillery or mortars. These HE rounds upon exploding sends shrapnel parallel to the ground.

The white phosphorous explodes like a large umbrella and drops straight down and sometimes land into the fighting hole. Any spot the WP hits will burn a hole straight through and it does not stop burning. A large amount can burn till about three or four inches deep has been exposed. The best result was to send a few rounds of WP into the area and hope some of the bad guys will get up to find cover then that is when you fire a bunch of HE into the area to try to get some of the bad guys while they are out of their holes. Fun is it not?

Here we go, day one; I slept in a hole next to my mortar. The hole dug for Sargent by Roks. About two am the sound of bugles and noise makers and shouting. OMG! here we go, "Fire Mission" is shouted into the radio by Lieutenant Lober. Everything is pitch black I cannot see any of the stakes. A direction is given on a map, these are coordinates used to determine position next a distance is given what do I do now? If I am short the shell will come into my front line. If I am too far to the right it may fall in on the Brits. Thank you, God, the Lt. shouts to me, I can hear his voice no need for a radio.

OMG! "Dago, get me some illumination here. (this round just explodes in the air like a giant fire cracker and lights up the area." Wow, what a relief; my first fire mission and it was a success and I know I had "nicotine in my trousers." Lesson learned!! In the future, I would leave my mortar set at about five hundred yards and O straight ahead through the middle of our front lines and about five-hundred-yard distance.

We are now advancing about twenty-five miles a day. We arrive in the Capitol City of Seoul. The usual search of all buildings for the nasty people.

Four of us arrive at Seoul University and went into a laboratory building. We have light back pack, rifle and helmets.

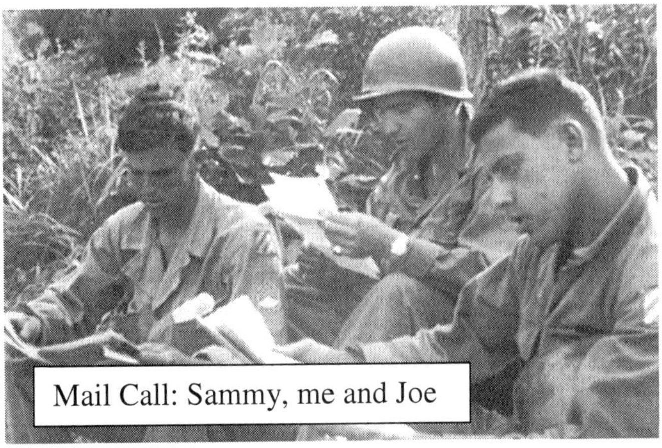

Mail Call: Sammy, me and Joe

We were a fierce bunch of warriors. Along a wall there was a bath tub of tile with a wooden cover on it. A long pole was sticking up from the top. We removed the wooden top and saw about five bodies in a chemical solution to preserve the cadavers for research. The long pole had a hook at the end to pull the bodies up. One of us fierce warriors accidently leaned onto the end of the pole. The movement caused a leg to go straight up. All four of us jerks, with equipment, jumped up and headed to the door and tried to charge through a thirty-inch opening. We all had a look of panic and started laughing at each other.

I am writing home as often as possible, I no longer called my mother Helen, its Mom. I send all my pay home. About $160.00 a month plus $45.00 combat pay and $10.00 per month for a combat infantry badge. This was a lot of money back then.

When I returned home in 1951, I found every penny of it in a savings account set up for me. After a month, the Red Cross got in touch with me to tell me that my father is worried he has not heard from me in a month. I will never know how he accomplished the things he did. God, I loved him. Also, I received a whole box of Snickers from my Mom, those did a number on my teeth. I made sure I wrote more often after that. This was to be one of two packages I received in one year. Mrs. Monfredo owned "Mary's Linen Shop" in our neighborhood at the corner of Montrose St. (another one of my surrogate mothers) Mary sent me a nice box of snacks and useful stuff. You better believe she was one of the first people I visited when I was discharged, lots of hugs and kisses for her whole family. In all fairness, all my surrogate mothers at this time were in their seventies or older. I would bet that I was in their prayers.

After Seoul, we were on a roll. We were promised home for Christmas so let's "lock and load" and get this over with. On the road north, fire fights occurred daily. Our first major skirmish was at the Majon-Ni perimeter. We tried to break through to hook up with the Brits. Korea was a United Nations affair, there were many countries taking part. It was important that you know who is on your left and right and their plans and their field of fire. It took a few days to get over the shock of combat. Finally, we adapted to the terrain and the enemies' style of engagement. Because of this skirmish, a few of our guys were awarded some very prestigious awards.

Our Field First Sergeant (three stripes on top and three rockers on bottom) was the highest-ranking NCO (non-commission officer). Sergeant Hopkins had only one more rocker than I but he was a hundred times better than I could ever dream of being. He served with the Brits during WWII and was our First Sergeant at Benning. Sergeant Hopkins was always the last to seek cover, and only after all his men were under cover. For this engagement, our company earned another battle star "Spring Offensive 1951."

Still able to laugh at a close call.
Note the bracelet.

The beginning of winter came on strong and the enemy got more aggressive.

Unfortunately, we could not protect the villagers and could only hope they would survive the winter. If we accomplished our goal of reaching the northern most boundaries, which was China, we would be home for Christmas.

Our 7th and 65th Regiments were on the east coast with our Marines. These units occupied Wonsan and Hamhung; our 15th Regiment was to their left. Little did we know that a task force more than 100,000 Chinese were preparing for an assault at the Korean border. It is now the first week in December and our battalion is at Chegyong with the goal to secure high ground at Songha-dong.

Our Regiment finally moved north through Hagaru and upwards toward the Frozen Changjin Reservoir; more commonly known as the "Frozen Chosin." During the first two weeks in December our Division was dispersed all over the place. The 65th and 7th were in place to protect our rear as we prepare for the largest military retreat ever. On or about the 15th of Dec. I remember looking across the Yalu River and seeing what appeared to be little ants by the thousands crossing into North Korea. OMG these were not ants, these were Chinese troops [later to be determined in total 225,000] entering to join in on the fun and games. Good-bye to "Home for Christmas," Hello Charlie Chan!!

On the 15th of December, we were hit by about four to five hundred Chinese Soldiers. The fire fight raged to four AM until the

Chinese retreated. We counted their dead at seventy-five and captured twenty prisoners. Although the Chinese had over twenty thousand in reserve they never attacked during the day for fear of our Naval and Air Power. I was good with a plotting board used to determine positions on a map and triangulations to determine the coordinates on a map for a Fire Mission from the Battleship Missouri about twenty miles away. These guys could place a sixteen-inch shell in your back pocket at twenty miles away. I hate to say it, but they put our artillery to shame. Now came the retreat we were to guard the rear of the Marine Division.

One night I helped to call for a fire mission from the Missouri. There was a small town we had to "take." Earlier in the day it was loaded with bad guys. To meet up with the "Brits" we had to go through this town.

This was beautiful yet frightening. These sixteen-inch shells passed over our heads coming down a few hundred yards ahead of us. This was precision, I was so proud that I could read the coordinates on the map.

Picture this, a huge ship tossing up and down in the water, yet the guns remained motionless and pointed in the right direction. The reason being, is the instrument called the gyroscope, keep guns on an even keel. (years later I found these to be the instrument I worked on at Bausch and Lomb). My boss there, was a genius at designing these instruments. The same principle is used on the gun of an army tank.

Next, the order was given to "move out," "lock and load" OMG! all we found was a dead dog.... The bad guys took off as soon as they realized what was going to happen. Even in war there must be an amount of humor.

During this time, it was called Chinese intervention, the temperatures at times went to forty-five degrees below zero. Many of us had severe frost bite hands, feet and faces. Our favorite past time was to stand near a fire and drink hot coffee. I hated coffee and melted snow for water. My guys wanted to shoot me because they became colder just looking at me.

This retreat at about twenty miles a day was a tough test. We had shoe packs for boots, your feet sweat during the day and froze during the night. The Marines were magnificent but lost many good kids in their efforts. These were just that, kids eighteen or nineteen years old.

As all troops arrived in Hamhung they were immediately loaded onto LCT's. These are landing craft troops. These boats ferried back and forth to the larger ships waiting to fill with about three to four thousand troops and re-deploy to Pusan so that we all can start over with the fun and games.

Our company was the last to leave Hamhung at 2:30 pm on hristmas Eve. We loaded from the first platoon to our fourth platoon. I was one of the five last men to leave. I appeared in many movie news programs and publications. This fact and five dollars may get me a Starbucks coffee. But being as I am a vain person I accept it graciously. Also on our boat were the engineers that placed the dynamite throughout the city. They blew up thousands of rounds of ammunition and all our Christmas dinners. The charges were on our boat and the engineers just had to push the levers as soon as ready. They waited till they saw the enemy start to admire their contraband. As soon as they saw a few hundred, they thought that was a bonus; the switches were compressed, and all old equipment and ammunition went up in a huge cloud of smoke. Also, included in this were a few hundred Chinese and all our Christmas dinners. This was sort of cool to watch the whole city implode.

The Navy did a magnificent job, kids again eighteen and nineteen driving these landing crafts in these rough seas. They got us to the ships for our journey to Pusan for the start over again.

Things were the Same 0, Same 0. One major difference was the draftees were starting to arrive; many came with experience gained in WW2.

Good "ole" Lt. Barns got a well-deserved medal today.

Chapter 4

A medical exam on board our ship determined that I would be transferred to the hospital ship for treatment for my severe frost bite. The Hospital ship was The Mercy, the one I was supposed to be a clerk on. Things were so confusing and I really wanted to get back to my platoon. Not because I was Gung Ho, but I was at least comfortable there and knew not where I could land if transferred.

Unfortunately, the Doctors of that time, did not realize how permanent the damage was to the nerves. I was told to get real woolen GI socks the itchier the better. This will be not only warm, but the psychology to your brain will be all that is needed while the healing is being finalized. In later years, the VA has discovered that frost bite damage was permanent. And …. I can attest to that; my feet and hands are cold 24/07.

The day I am leaving I have mixed emotions
No more foxholes, mud and cold "C" rations.
Hand shakes, back slappin and "stay in touch I am told."
But Dear God most of all, I remember the cold.

I peer out my window and see the snow fall
I see determined, staunch warriors standing tall.
We fought and won battles in God awful places
What troubles me now is I can't put names to faces.

Charlie "The Hawk" from Fall River, Mass.
The guy from Ohio, got a "Dear John" from his Lass.
That big Dude from Texas, who said "Howdy," never hello
Claimed his ancestors fought at the Alamo.

Our hair has turned gray now, our pace not so fast
But it does not diminish our glorious past.
Time is the artist that has drawn our faces old
But most of all I remember the cold.

A poem by John Lennox, S/Sgt Able Battery
10th F.A. Third Infantry. Division. 1950-1951.

Now I start my trek back to our Charlie Company. Here we go again back up north, it's now January 1951." And a Happy New Year to you also." I start the walk in my flashy new itchy socks; at least we were a lot south of the frozen Chosen. Where ever we went there were remains of the wasted land, buildings and all the wreckage of war. The thing I remember most, was when we first arrived in Korea, there were remnants of destroyed enemy tanks and other vehicles that some GI's wrote in white paint "this tank destroyed by Major General Dean." I can only imagine what those first ones in must have gotten into. Can you believe it, a General shoulder to shoulder with a bunch of kids eighteen to twenty-one years old on the line knocking out a tank?

It was our custom to set out guards every evening; Sargent of the Guard would check on everyone every half hour. Weather was not as bad as it was at the Chosin, but it would go to zero at night. The drill was three hours on than three hours off. Most homes [more like mud houses] all had a large stack about twenty feet high of rice stalks more like a heavy grass. If you burrowed in a way it was as warm and comfortable as you would ever need. Private Dan Innoye from Hawaii (no relation to the Senator) fell asleep for his three-hour duty; Sargent Hopkins pulled a pin on a grenade and ask him to hold it with both hands and now it would be OK for him to fall asleep. Enough said about that.

The Army teaches its soldiers to adapt to any situation and prepares you for most emergencies. A few months later we did not have a base camp. Meaning, no makeshift shower or hot food or clean water, we carried chlorine base tablets to put into our canteen if we filled on any water not cleaned by our own mess Sargent. Our Company was really on a fast pace to get back up North.

My Ammo Carrier Sang Soo Kim, goes running into a field and came out eating a cold juicy "apple." I was given one of the bluish color turnip, it was great cold juicy, I swear I burped that taste for over six months. [ugh ugh]. Later at night we bivouacked on a small mountain top. Still thirsty I spotted a great stream on top of the mountain. I made a huge mistake, instead of filling the canteen and add two pills and wait a minute, I put my head in the stream and drank heartily. The other twenty, thirty guys did the same. Little did we know that a mile upstream a large battle was fought; a lot of nasty stuff was left in that stream.

Because of this act of stupidity, I started out with dysentery then to make matters worse Type C jaundice. I was not sent back to a hospital but was treated by our battalion medics. Not too bad, I followed our guys wherever they went; only I was driven in an ambulance wherever we went. Not only did I look yellow but I lost over twenty-five pounds. I was weak and had to go to the" John" every hour or so, this lasted for three weeks. Finally, I return to my outfit. Murph Berardi from Rochester in the rear {Artillery} was dug in and I got to say hello and visit while waiting for transportation to my outfit. Murph broke down and cried. I cherished the picture taken of us for years. Sorry to say, it was lost in one of my moves later with Allstate.

I am now promoted to Sgt. 1st. Class. This is the second highest non-commissioned officer NCO. This promotion puts three Sargent's, three corporals, and thirty Ammo bearers under my command. Not too shabby for a skinny kid from the Green Grass. A lot of responsibility and I am overwhelmed, but I had a lot of help from Corporal Gooley. The Corporal just had so much knowledge he gained in WW2. I also learned so much from Sam Jarrell also a SFC, but is now ready to go home. This is the "revenuer" that could not read, but man he knew his weapons. In civilian life, he later became a pastor.

At night, we would dig in. We always dug a five-foot circle for the mortar and room for the gunner and assistant gunner; ammunition was placed along the outside the ammo carriers would dig theirs before we bedded down for the night.

One night after a long march to catch up with some of the guys that advanced maybe twenty miles, we were to relieve them the next day so we were still in the rear and no need to set up for firing just rest until told to "rock and roll" or "lock and load," either one meant get your fanny in high gear and move out. 0500 hours the call came all my guys know the drill and all played follow the leader. "What Leader?" I was still asleep in the hole I built for myself all cuddled and warm. About eight am I woke to find the hill deserted.... OMG! What to do now!! I was dressed in a heavy white Parka with no sign of identification. I ran to the bottom of the hill nothing but snow and ice. Fortunately, I guessed right I turned left and followed the hill around for a mile or so. Oh NO! A jet F50 is circling above me. I only hoped he came down low enough to see that I was only a straggler, Finally, I spotted my outfit and I just slid among my men as if nothing really happened. The ROKS did not have a clue on what happened. So, there was no need to burden anyone.

Each day brings me closer to my discharge date of September 7th and departure from Korea 30 days prior. We are now into March, Same O Same O.... I received a letter one day from a young lady in Rochester. Dear Frank, you don't know me but would you please send me a letter as if we know each other. I am five foot five, blonde hair and appreciate if you can say something like "I hope you are well and will see you soon etc. Another OMG, I call Lt. Lober, and asked how long does it take to have a baby? "About nine months." Well that's good so, it cannot be me. What to do now?

As was the drill we all carried a candle in our pocket. If we could have light and a little warmth in the hole a candle was a must. I once saw in a movie a King sealed a document with wax and imprinted his ring into the hot wax. So, I put the letter back into the envelope, melted the wax over the fold and wrote a note to my Dad. "Do not open until I return home or if I am killed. Here we go again the Red Cross gets in touch. How the hell was my father able to get these people to contact me...? I would not know where to start. Ok I know the drill, come down from your perch and go back to Headquarters to speak to the RC. "Hi Sgt., Borrelli, we understand that you have had a little problem from a lady back home?" Not again, my Dad opened my letter and I told him not to. Nothing more on that subject after I claimed complete innocence and all will be taken care of as soon as I return home.

The 23 of March 1951, our orders were to take hill 322 at a place called WI Jong Bu. This area was needed for our supply routes to our forward divisions. Forward was more East and West than North. Our lines were all on the same parallel. This was to be our first major conflict with the strength of the Chinese Army. At this point the Chinese were at a full complement of troops. They were well equipped with Infantry. Also mortars and rockets. This was to be our "World Series" of 1951.

General of The Armies Douglas McArthur was present at the bottom of the Hill. We were through with our fire mission so we just watched as our guys followed a few of our tanks up the hill. This was not much fun for our troops. There were four DSM's given out this day. [Distinguished Service Cross is the 2nd highest medal, second only to The Medal of Honor] This is unheard of but the big man was there to help things along.

One of our men had a rather large spread nose. My nick name was Sgt. Dago and his was "major Nose" he really was only a private." I witnessed all of this, WOW it's just like in the movies suddenly Major Nose bayonets a Chinese in a hole that lead to a tunnel. He virtually lifted the man up and out of the hole. The General hollers "give that man a Silver Star". That is a nice award a little more common than the DSM but.... The Chinese was already dead when Nose bayoneted him. But they all did a great job. I really was glad that I did not have to lug that 57MM recoilless rifle up that hill. This is another perk to being a mortar man.

The recipients of the DSM that day were: Sgt. Weaver, Lt. Dodson, Sgt. Bales, Lt. Barnes and Sgt. Callahan. Sgt. Bales was a good friend when I was with the 57MM; he remained and did himself proud that day. Personally, I think the show for the General must have pumped everyone up. five DSM's for one engagement is rare. But it was a great offensive move for our side.

April to August 1951

After the fun and games at Uijongbu, it was my turn at R & R. Rest and relaxation was always something to look forward to. One week in Japan. My destination was Osaka a port city. I buddied up with a draftee that was a top drummer of that time his name was Bobby Johns. I don't remember too much other than the Shrimp was outstanding and the Ashai beer was great. The Saki was too much for me to handle. Another note was there were no cars except a few taxis. Gas was nonexistent; all cars had a small furnace attached to the rear bumper. The engines were converted to steam engines; and the furnace was to create the steam necessary to drive the engine.

There was a good reason for me to behave while on R and R. One was that I was close to my D day; another was the previous month a friend from B Company was trying for more medals than our former member of the 15th Reg., Audie Murphy {the most decorated soldier in history}. My friend was to get a fantastic award; he was to go to DC and try out for a guard of the Unknown Soldier. As he was given a medical inspection, it was determined that he contacted a virus while in Japan. I thought he was too short for the Honor Guard anyway.

I have now returned to my outfit and its "Same O, Same O." A few fire fights nothing too exciting. But someone always seems to get hurt. It is now the beginning of August I had passed the thirty-day period and getting nervous. I am not only worried about the bad guys so much it is something now called {friendly fire} I sincerely believe that 50% of all casualties in Korea were from our own Artillery or Airforce. We lost over 50,000 beautiful "kids" in Korea…I am now feeling a nervous fear never felt before. Man, I was saying prayers like never before. I want home and the green Grass and girls in "bobby socks" and the beach. The picture I sent home on Christmas Eve and ask my mother to have it put in the local newspaper "to be sure girls know I am still alive" did work a little. I received a few encouraging letters from home and surrounding areas. This was so appreciated and formed a core of my first calls when I got home. I still have revenge in mind when I return.

OMG! At 0230 bugles and noise makers and shouts; we are hit big time. Our tracer's bullets are a red-hot bullet, the Chinese have a bright green bullet. Now I look up and above my head is a barrage of red tracers coming over head. Uh oh; they overran our machine gunners and have turned our own guns on us. I am now praying out loud in case God missed my first call. I am supposed to be on my way home ten days ago. I know I am liked but that can go just so far. Suddenly I heard a low chant "retreat." Omg, what sweet words we have never been kicked off a mountain, or never have not held our position in a year. We had no choice the bad guys are between our ranks.

Adelino Flores was sharing my hole; we were unable to look over the top of the hole we started shaking with fear so bad that our steel helmets were hitting each other's. Never in the past year had I known fear such as this; yes, we were praying out loud. Once again, all I can say is "Thank You Jesus!" My platoon slid down almost the entire mountain with our mortars and all ammo. About two hundred yards downhill was a road, where we regrouped until our friends the Turks went into a night mode and retook the hill. I gained a lot of respect for these soldiers.

We all sat on that road for enough time to allow our guys to join us. A roll call was taken, my whole mortar section" was present and accounted for." Now the word to move out is given to us. We are to regroup and relieve the Turks in the morning. My friend God was with me again. The second person on my right was our machine gunner. A 30-caliber air cooled machine gun has a pistol grip trigger it is exposed. Apparently, the gunner picked the gun up by the barrel and the trigger caught on a traverse bar between the two legs of the bipod. Unfortunately, the Gunner failed to clear his piece and there was a round in the chamber. God was there again for me; the bullet went to the left and struck Pvt. Jones on his right temple and continued left to pass within two inches of my face. The private fell at my feet and to this day I can hear his fluids run out as from a gallon bottle being emptied.

I am now about twenty days to discharge. God please do not let me go back. We are in the rear, a mile from the fun and games. A call comes; "Rock and Roll", move out at 0800. Then out of the blue there comes a final call "Sargent Borrelli, bag and baggage;" oh what wonderful words.

Homeward Bound August 1951

Throughout the year, we were told that we were not to take any souvenirs home. Apparently to do so would cause major delays and possible charges. This proved wrong no one ever checked my bags. So, I guess it did work and very few people brought trophies home.

Along with the sad goodbyes I gave my ROK friends anything of value. To Sang soo kim I gave my wrist watch; A beautiful Russian 25cal. Pistol (taken off of a Chinese Officer) to one of my squad leaders. That's about all I owned not much need for anything of value.

Fellow comrades came from all Companies and we were all to be shipped to a" Repo Depo." Sargent was singled out and ordered to report to regimental. Now what? Always fear the worst then you can handle any disappointment. I was offered a field commission of Warrant Officer. Apparently, all Master Sergeants that may have been qualified refused, and I was next in line. Of course, this would mean re-enlistment for another 3 years. The skinny kid from the Green Grass was honored. A Warrant Officer rates a salute but is usually in Logistics such as Supply or Motor pool. I think that clerk school I went to was a part of my record and helped after all. I respectfully declined; I just want to go home.

The first night in the Repo Depo we were issued a hot shower and all new clothes even white under shirts. Wow our undershirts were always olive drab. White is not very good to be wearing at night. Now nothing to do but hurry up and wait that is the Army. That night "bed check Charlie" came by. A small plane circles our tents. This bad guy Chinese flying close to the ground drops hand grenades out the window. We all got the hell out of the tents to seek cover; off came all the white shirts. One guy ran too far and fell into

a Rice Paddy loaded with Honey buckets of human waste used for fertilizer. **Autres temps-autres moeurs,** this is for sure.

Finally, we move out on trucks to Pusan for our Embarkation to the good Ole USA 19 August 1951, arrival in Pusan. We arrived one year ago and were excited not frightened, admired all the girls not in total but they all had pretty legs. To sum up the situation we were once attached to the French Foreign Legion. These guys were all good looking worldly about ten years older than our average. A Sargent mentioned to me that he has dated women all over the world, but in a million years he would not get near any of these girls. That's another "Temp." There was no hygiene when we arrived it was nothing but a huge dust bowl even in the winter there was dust everywhere. Now that's a different Country and their good looks can be appreciated.

Now for our ten-day trip to Seattle and then on to home. We boarded about thirty-five-hundred of us on a troop ship at Pusan Harbor. I won about $800.00 playing black jack on the floor or deck of the ship. Not too shabby. There were eager hands looking for a loan once we arrived in Seattle.

Our ship docked about the 31st day of August. I have never seen a welcome like that. There were at least ten thousand at the dock. There were great likenesses for each Division. The 1st Calvary had a broom and shovel against the fence, the 7th Division had an hour glass, our 3rd Division had a huge rock....we are known as the Rock of the Marne. I cannot remember them all but there were at least a dozen articles.

We were greeted by at least fifty thousand people little did we know that the hype was out because we had on board the 10,000th

A Great Welcome

serviceman returning from Korea. As we were disembarking I noticed a convertible with a gorgeous girl in it. This woman gets out while troops are going down the gang plank and continues to within a few feet. She is about twenty feet away OMG! she is here to meet me. My father must have called the Red Cross again. She walks closer and puts her arm around the fellow two in front of me; he is number 10,000 I am 10,002. This was Yolanda Betbetze Miss America 1950. Miss America was this GI's date for the day and evening.

We were loaded on buses and came down the main drag of Seattle.

OMG! girls galore by the hundreds welcoming us running to the busses to shake hand and throw kisses. We arrive at Camp Stockton after a short ride.

I am memorizing the route. After dark about five of us found a dark spot and jumped the fence. I had about $500.00 left and this is a lot of money in 1951. We catch a cab and proceeded to town to latch on to one of the thousand girls we spotted earlier.

When we arrive in town there was not even a street cleaner. It was now about 9 o'clock and the town was deserted. So as is the case with most of the cab drivers, they know where the action is. Our driver takes us to a country hideaway. This was territorial. Girls started to peel off and flirt leaving the guys they were with. I learned a few things on the Green Grass along with the time spent in Phoenix City Al. There was a movie made called" The Phoenix City Story." This was considered the toughest town in the USA. Rumor had it that General Patton took one of his tanks to town and demanded they release some of his men or suffer the consequences. His Tank Division was shipping out and he was not going to lose a few men to these yokels.

Knowing we were going home the next day we decided to call it a night and return to base; except for one guy Richard, he asked me to loan him a hundred dollars he was in love. There was no way we could get him out of there. Returning to camp was something, we could not go through the gate we had no identification. Somehow, we managed to talk the guard into letting us in. I remember more about age five than that night but we were safe at home for now.

Any port in the storm.

Next morning, we woke up to a loud speaker to report to the parade grounds for instructions. We were all going to various camps nearer to our homes. In my case, I am going back to Ft. Dix. Suddenly a disheveled Richard Baker appears he looked like he had a hangover on some kind of drug. Apparently, he had a good time drinking with his new love the last he remembers he woke up propped up at a tree with a note and $3.00 "this is for cab fare back to camp." I never saw him again, nor my $100.00 again.

I arrive at Fort Dix on the 4th of September, a ton of examinations and physicals and paper work. Armies are all the same, rumors abound like weeds. I was told to tell the final examiner nothing or my discharge will be delayed. My turn in line, I am asked if I had any injuries or sick time? I answered that I never lost a day and feel great. A gentleman with a small desk on the lawn was one of about twenty-five advocates for returning GI's. Most were from VFW and

American Legion and Red Cross. This guy comes up to me and says to come by his desk to talk. "Cut the shit, and tell me all about any of your sick time." I repeat to him what I had heard; not to talk to anyone. This guy I owe my marriage and sanity to, he made a complete case for me and came to Rochester to represent my case to the VA.

While waiting for my final release, back pay, mustering out pay of $200.00 and my Honorable Discharge, and final run down of my record including my Sergeant rate but a permanent Corporal rating. Field commissions are all temporary, unless you reenlist and bargain for the rank as an incentive or bonus to re-up.

While at Fort Dix, I spend most of my time at the PX. There is a pinball machine and while playing, I tell the guy I am playing against that at Al's Stand across the street from the Green Grass there is a guy that is the best at pin ball machines, Fred Traci. As I turn next to the doorway there is Freddie he is a recruit that just got drafted OMG!! Freddie!! Come over here and show this guy for me. After a few hugs, we had a crowd of at least twenty guys watching and Freddie cleaned up a few dollars. Now I go to the mess hall and see a kid I graduated with John Dawson he just got drafted and was on KP duty. Don't worry John, I can get you off KP. Wrong, I had new fatigues not tailored and no stripes put on but I still feel like and am a Sergeant. I pleaded with the mess Sgt. and he was non-sympathetic. Oh well John I tried.

Next morning my first commercial flight from Newark to Rochester. Sitting in the last row was "Dynamite" Bradacurti, a friend from Rochester. Oh Boy! Its starting, I am getting to see familiar people and places. I had butterflies in my stomach and about $250.00 in my pocket. Arrive at about 11:00 am to hugs and kisses. I cannot wait to get started as a civilian.

OMG! Another reason to be surprised by my dad; this man never ceased to amaze me. My mom Helen, and dad had a baby girl on the day I left Korea. I really march to a different drum. Teresa Marie my little sister was twenty years younger, but was old enough to be our flower girl at our wedding. So, after we had our two children, Teresa Maria was a big aunt but not old enough to be called "aunt". So, my dad now had Frankie for his fishing partner and Theresa Marie and Carol Ann to entertain. Teresa Maria was the bossy older sister and we all grew up together. It was a great time and I think my mom did a great job keeping all in line.

MEMORIAM

..... In chambered temples of silence the dust of their dauntless valor sleeps, waiting, waiting in the chancery of heaven the final reckoning of Judgement Day. 'Only those are fit to live who are not afraid to die'..."

General Douglas Mac Arthur

To my fallen brethren;

My thanks to all of you that helped me make my transition from "A skinny kid" to An adult. May God be with you always!

Charlie Company

15th. Infantry Regiment

Sgt Amigh, Harry Lewis ....28 Nov 50
Pvt Bellow, Glen E. ....31 Mar 52
Pvt Black, James W. ....24 Feb 52
Cpl Boger, Leonard J. ....31 Jan 51
1st Lt Camp, Henry C. Jr...........13 Feb 51
Cpl Collins, Jack L. ....24 May 51
Pvt Correll, Daniel A. ....24 May 51
Pvt Davis, Robert A. ....25 Mar 51
Pvt Day, Glen R. ....24 May 51
Pvt Delgado, Rudolfo Jr............ 4 Oct 51
1st Lt Dinkel, Jack L. V. ....24 Jun 51
Capt Everett, Harry S. Jr.......... 8 Mar 51
Cpl Farnham, Glenn W. .... 4 Oct 51
Pfc Fouchey, Bernard E. ....22 Sep 51
Cpl Freeman, Theron H. ....25 May 51
Pfc Glasgow, Ralph N. ....22 Sep 51
SFC Jennings, Robert L. .... 4 Jun 51
Cpl Johnson, Andy C. .... 4 Oct 51
Pvt Jones, Charlie ....17 Aug 51
Pfc Leon-Guerrero, Jose G. ....15 Feb 52
Sgt Munsey, Roy L. .... 4 Oct 51
Cpl Ortiz, Ismael ....17 Aug 51
Cpl Peralta, Joseph C. ....25 Mar 51
Cpl Piskolti, Albert ....24 Jun 51
Pvt Reyes-Rivera, Luis ....17 Aug 51
Pvt Stebbins, George F. ....24 May 51
Pvt Taylor, Joe D. ....31 Jan 51
Pfc Velazquez, Jorge ....29 Sep 51
Pfc Wise, Paul ....24 May 51
Pvt Woods, Earl E. .... 7 Jun 51

My last day was 18 Aug, 1951 note the names on the 17 Aug.

THE START OR CONTINUATION OF MY CIVILIAN LIFE

I am not sure what car I used but I did have a license to drive. While on leave in 1950, Vito Carrichio my very dear friend taught me how to drive. I was terrible, I remember while learning in the parking lot another learner and I collided. To this day, I think it was 50/50 at fault. Vito had no insurance and the father of the driver hollered we were at fault but he would accept $200.00. I immediately went to my father and asked for $200.00; I remember that he did not ask what it was for but gave me money from the "Budget book." My father earned then, about $475.00 per week. Once again, I had occasion to be proud of my Dad; but felt awful. About fifteen years later while visiting Vito in his home in California he reminded that the driver of the other car was Tom, my wife's old boyfriend, but by then all was forgotten.

I think it was my dad's car I could use that first day. So, off I go to the other side of town to visit my letter writer. At about two pm I knocked on the door, this cannot be her, she is at home. Apparently, she was unemployed or working nights. "Hi, Frank, won't you come in." This cannot be possible I never seen this person in my lifetime. "I suppose you want to find out about the letter I sent you." I asked that question of me many times. Now maybe I will have an answer.

This was an uncomfortable place to be especially because she was a cute girl about twenty-five at most and I would turn twenty the next day. I did not want even a glass of water I had no way of knowing what I got into. I figured someone was going to come out of the woodwork any minute. Apparently, this young lady was having an affair with my mother's husband. My "real mother," we don't want to confuse this situation with my dad or my mother Helen. My mother had a detective on "Mary" 24/7. Several months prior, I had a large picture in the local paper; Jim cut it out to show "Mary." Jim told her that this was a picture of his wife's son. Mary thought if she could show that we were friends Jim would have to break it off. Jim did not want this affair to end, and I really could care less. I made my position clear that I had not seen my mother for over fifteen years and I also felt that I did not want to be involved in any way. Mary would have to figure this one out for herself. Goodbye and Sayonara Jo San.

That was it and I was proud I made no moves on the individual. It's now close to five pm and I finally am going home to a dinner. No sooner do I enter the house, but my father yells across the table. "And where were you today" I said, "I went down town to look at some clothes." What are you talking about? You went to see that "putana."

How in the hell could he have found out? Apparently, the detective still had Mary under surveillance, and recognized the soldier arriving at the house. The detective immediately called my mother; she in turn calls my Aunt Angie, apparently, they remained friends. My Aunt picks up the phone and calls my father to ask if he knew that his son Jr. was visiting the girl Mary. My father was so happy to see me home safe and sound that hewould have forgiven me almost anything.

Now I must go to my "to do list" and start the check off process. First, I better stay home and get some sleep tonight.

Nonno Joe wakes me up the next morning; "Junuo" [junior] get up you go to work with me today." OMG, I hand carry four hundred blocks to him and four hundred blocks to Angelo in this huge cellar pit for a home they were building. Each of these two elderly gents would lay this many cement blocks a day before they quit for the day. I was the only helper I had to keep mixing mortar for them and follow to supply blocks as needed. Every fifteen minutes, "Junuo more mud, Junuo more block," I am dead ... about four pm a truck delivers about five hundred blocks. At that time, they delivered to the site and slid the blocks into the hole. The helper grabs two at a time and stacks them onto the four sides of the cellar. The inside of both arms became raw and I thought my back was broken. The next day Nonno Joe comes into my bedroom; "Junuo, get up we go to work". Nonno Joe, "I quit."

Wonders of the world my mother gives me a savings account book. I cannot believe every penny I sent home was saved $4,700.00. That is one heck of a lot of money.

LET'S GO SHOPPING

First a car and then clothes. Dad knows a lot of people at Ralph Pontiac so I purchased a brand-new Pontiac sedan. One week later I decided it was not for me I paid $1,299.00 for it new; but there was the sharpest one of the year a 1952 Pontiac Catalina. Total cost was about $1,900.00. I purchased this great car two tone green and white, it was a hard-top convertible. It was a two door with visor and no upright window tracks. This was the sharpest now, it would be worth ten times that. Next clothes, must have blue suede shoes and black peg pants also a one button roll double breasted suit.

Now I am all set to meet the rest of the world. What happened to all the "bobby socks?" All the girls are wearing heels and short dresses. "Thank God, peg pants are still in." The only civvies from Ft. Benning were a pink shirt, one pair of peg pants and blue suede shoes.

No one sits on the Green Grass any more. Al's Stand is still selling the ice lemonade and hot dogs. There is a different kind of cliental hanging out at Al's Stand. A lot of the guys my age had been drafted, Korea is still going strong, and I am calling a lot of my comrades almost daily. No cell phones in those days, it was pay as you call, and boy did I get socked with the long-distance charges. The biggest change at Al's Stand was the removal of the pinball machines. The nicest change was that girls now hung out there with the guys. These girls were young kids when I left, now they were over eighteen some maybe twenty. Wow I was just 21 and thought I died and went to heaven. This was like having my own harem. No more bobby socks and I am outnumbered by five to one, not too shabby. The big hang out in those days was the Edgerton Grill where I set pins as a kid. Now I am old enough to drink and hang out at the bar. OMG, one night I walk into the side door with a few of the gang and see a guy at the bar with pink pants on. Smart ass me wants to know who the man is with the pink pants on. He turns and its Rocky Marciano, the Heavyweight Champ now what do I do? He looks and laughs and I buy his party a drink and shake his hand. Paul Borregine brought him to town; he was appearing with Jane Mansfield at a lounge in Albion.

Now I enter a new part of my life. Unprepared, under educated, few friends (most are now employed or have been drafted into the service) my dear friend Larry Catalo died the day I left for service. Fortunately, I visited him the day before he passed. But on the positive side, I am no longer the skinny kid from the Green Grass. Now I am not a giant but at five foot nine and one-hundred sixty pounds, of great conditioned no fat, with confidence and at least able to settle a few grudges.

First things first, the letter writer and that's out of the way. I must not forget to visit Mary's Linen Shop; Mary Monfredo sent me the only Christmas present I received. Mrs. Monfredo was a fixture in the neighborhood. In those days so many people sewed and made things crocheted or knitted were things of beauty.

On day two my Aunt Teresa and the "Roncone Girls" had it all arraigned someone had a niece twenty years old and this would be a great match. This young lady was very cute but I had too much to accomplish before I enter a relationship. Why not? I agreed to play Boy Scout and arraigned a date for the next evening. I was a perfect gentleman and called for her about seven pm held the door for all to see what a gentleman I was. We drove out to the Flyers Club near the Airport for a lite bite and a drink. While waiting for the waiter we looked at each other and burst out laughing. Both of us knew that this was a put up and what do we do now or next. We enjoyed our "seven and seven" the drink of new drinkers and had a great time just laughing. We never dated again but are dear friends to this day. We both realized that we were "oil and water" and no way would it work. It must have been a nice date.

Despite the fun and games, we had in Korea; there was a lot of time spent on thinking. Most of my thoughts were of home and the nice things that happened to me. These were embellished along with any of my accomplishments though they be very few and surely nothing to brag about. Revenge was also in my thoughts. These thoughts were a positive because they helped me stay awake when it was needed. One thing always bothered me most. On the Library steps one rainy day "Mentels" "sucker punched" me. My nose was bleeding like a water fountain I think it was broken. I did not cry but I went home [to an empty house] and was angrier at myself for not getting even. Now, I was about thirteen years old.

Sometime in October, after a night of drinking, about five or six of us went to our favorite late-night Greek restaurant; called The Northway, in the Bull's Head area. Anthony made a remark about someone in our gang and that gave me the reason. This person could not shine the shoes of the people I lived with, hanged with, prayed with and fought alongside with. **"Autres temps, autres moeurs."** the Army taught us to kill not fight, I had maniacal strength I could feel no pain. Thank God, Sonny Giuliano and a few other friends broke it up. I only remember Sonny because his hand was in my mouth while he pulled me off. I am no longer "The Skinny Kid from the Green Grass." Two years later I attended his wedding. I have not seen him since; that's what also happens when you marry an eastsider.

The next day, I was driving down Saratoga Ave. and I spot one of the girls that shared our blankets at the beach. Nice person but friends; serious stuff I doubt. Hey girl, how are you, where you are going? Just hanging out, it's been a long time, let's go have a drink down by the lake. We went to Island Cottage bar and Restaurant on Beach Ave. My friend Mike Di Lella was the bartender. This is 1951 and $30.00 is like $125.00 now.

We were at the restaurant about an hour and I am told not to call her again. This threw me for a loop until she explained. "I am in love with someone and I just have to wait until he realizes that he loves me" Great, little did I know that her fantasy was ready to get engaged to another local. So, it's decided let's call it an evening. The waiter brings a bill for four drinks, $29.50. OMG, I waited till the waiter was on the other side of the room and dropped the $30.00 on the table and walked out like I owned the place. I know there was a mistake and I could have borrowed a few dollars from Mike tending bar, but this was too embarrassing; especially after the brush off. I did her a major favor inviting her for a drink any way. Later it was determined that I would stick with my neighborhood friends.

CHAPTER 5

Later that week I received a call from the VFW. My appointment for disability with the VA will be in 3 days. (Veterans Administration on State Street).

After a complete physical, I was awarded various service connected disabilities, some of these were not to include compensation others a percentage of 100% disability. It is important to have everything on record, because some ailments may become troublesome in the future. Dollar amount now for 60% was about $75.00. Today that would amount to over one thousand dollars, that's 1951 vs. 2017 over sixty years ago.

Next to the Education Department, all GI's receive college tuition. Any disabled veterans under public law sixteen received at that time six years of college, and all books, with $110.00 per month spending money and housing. I agreed that I wanted to go to college. When asked what college, I responded "I want to go to the University of Miami." I was told to cut the shit and that my choice is between University of Buffalo and the University of Syracuse, furthermore I must go for three days of testing to see if I can make the grade.

After testing on Ohio State Physiological Exams, and a few others, it was determined that I could study at the 2nd year level of college. I enrolled in the University of Buffalo and was accepted. Next, I met with the president of the Business school. He looks me straight in the eye and informed me as follows. "Young man you have passed your entry exams; one thing I must inform you is that we do not wear peg pants or blue suede shoes here." Now, in my life, I still respected all my elders. God only knows what I wanted to tell him. The fact this former skinny kid from the Green Grass had five stripes and the lives of forty soldiers in his "care, custody and control."

I just left his office and remember a long sidewalk to the street and next to this was the new dorm that Lou Bommate had waiting for me as his roommate.

Finally, I arrive home and discussed this with my Dad. His reply was "you are earning $80.00 a week at Bausch and Lomb and you have a new car all paid for, what the hell do you want to go to college for?" This kind of guidance is not what I needed. My option was to go to night school at the U of R. This was great because in those days the U of R was not co-ed.

The Continued Ed Dept. was at the Girls Campus on Prince Street and University Ave. Not too many college kids owned cars; too bad, whenever on Friday nights the school would have "mixers" (school dance with students from The Eastman School of music preforming). Not too shabby there were girls galore waiting to be asked to dance. And my former upstairs neighbor on 21 Montrose St. was the person in charge. Angie Dinuzzio was a dear friend that had graduated from the U of R and worked in their Personnel Dept. She and her younger sister Viola were two very bright students that helped the school average at Jefferson; where only about 5% went on to continue their education.

NOW TO THE REAL WORLD
(work and more work)

Here is a chronological list of the jobs needed to survive. I averaged at least two jobs at a time and pursued a college degree [almost achieved but lacked about another year full time]

1951 to 1954: Bausch and Lomb and night school; I tried doing two subjects Monday and Wednesday night four hours two subjects. For two weeks at night Western Auto, this was a learning experience in sales. 1954 I opened a Jewelry Store closed in 1956, too much credit and there were no credit cards at that time.

1954 to 1960: Full time United States Postal Service continued night school. I also worked a 2nd job for these six years. This would be three commitments weekly.

John Antonelli paid a visit to the Post Office
Notice the original IKE jacket style.

During these six years, my part time jobs were; Taxi Driver 1954 to 1957, hustled jewelry for all these year's. In 1957, a life saver came into my life, Hiram Fitch, owner of Fitch Furniture needed a part time Salesperson to relieve his full-time sales people for dinner. Fantastic, this allowed me to go through a correspondence school and still work full time at the post office. And I never missed one of my son's baseball games. My post office truck could always be seen on the edge of the outfield. Also, along with the jewelry I was selling, I also sold mattresses from 1954 to 1960. This was great income; dad ran the furniture warehouse for Fitch and in the same building was the Sealy Mattress Company. So, my father the salesman, was an established account there. There will be more about these jobs later.

1960 to 1998 THE BIG LEAGUES

After being refused by Allstate three times, I finally was hired by Mr. Jack Gossin. On the third try, I felt I had nothing to lose. Previous times I went with my great winter coat blue Cashmere and double-breasted suit. This time the same type Cashmere beige still with the cuff links but a vested three button suit. When asked what I thought it would take to be hired, I answered "all I should do is impress you and I am golden, and that is a piece of cake."

I was hired and went to Jamestown for three weeks of study to pass the NYS exam for Casualty Insurance. We worked eight hours a day in class at Jamestown Community College. The instructor was an owner of a large agency and had a fantastic average of students that passed the State exam. I passed and became an agent on the 12th of June. This date later became very important.

My starting salary was $450.00 per month guaranteed or commission, whichever is the greater. Currently with my two jobs I am earning about $650.00 a month. My commission for the remainder of the two weeks was over $700.00. Never did I ever go less than $2,500.00 per month plus residuals.

1967 to present: I started to purchase rental property. In 1973, I started with my "compare" Fulvio, a builder and his brother Angelo. My credit was good, so I parleyed the first to the 2nd to the 3rd to the 4th and then 5th. Money was easy to get in those days. Within two months we owned five large houses on Lake Ave. Like magic, the houses became five to as many as nine studio apartments. Total apartments were forty within a year. About five years later we split and sold the properties. I learned a great deal from Fulvio, and later started buying condos in Florida.

1968: Angelo Felice asked me to join him in a new travel agency on Lyell Ave we called it Universal Travel. Automation with computer reservation systems was available in 1970. Angelo did not see the benefits of this. So, I agreed to buy him out or he could buy me out. Angelo bought me out and I started Borrelli Travel at The Lincoln Bank Building.

1970 to 2015: Full time travel agency. Borrelli Travel was sold in 2015 for $250,000.00, our gross annual sales were about four million. Along this time, I started a Travel Agent School in our agency. Later I was asked to start a program for St. John Fisher College. Along with my staff, I taught at Fisher from 6pm to 9pm. We all did this for six years then it became a little too much.

This course was certified by the accredited certification school in Wesley Massachusetts. Each student when finished with the five courses of study received a certification as a travel agent. Almost all that were looking for jobs were successful including dozens hired by the local airlines at the Rochester Airport.

Reed Hoffmann Democrat and Chronicle
Frank Borrelli, who heads an area training program for travel agents.

1968 to 1970: Delfay Charter Tours. Mike Delfay asked me if I would go in partnership with him in chartering groups to Vegas. So, I moved it to my basement and put my lovely current Bonaventure graduate daughter in law Ann in charge. Mike was a "Bank," this is the guy that controls all the money that the bookies take in and pay out. I have no idea how it works but he was a cool dude. Mike would walk into the office of the president of Caesars Palace or any of the hotels in Vegas and control the conversation. Each plane we brought in had two hundred and fifty "High Rollers" we would bring in six of these a year. And I don't even gamble.

I get nervous if I win, and nervous if I lose. I worked too hard to give it all to a Casino. Part of any education in life, is not always gained by books or school. Mike had in his hands millions of dollars daily, this does not mean that he has credit ranking in the seven or eight hundred marks. In fact, Mike could not go to an insurance company and purchase a bond needed to do business with the charter airlines. Conversely, I had no money but my credit rating was excellent. This might be because I had good income and was able to prove it. I guess I could live with various financial commitments and make payments on time. Also, a job with insurance you must be able to secure a Fiduciary Bond for yourself. So, Mr. Frank went to a bank in Syracuse and signed an agreement for three charters to Vegas; ninety thousand dollars. We were now bonded and in business.

Prior to running charters to Vegas, Mike owned a gambling joint on Lyell Ave. called the Lyell Social Club.This is plus being a bank for all the "wanna be's," small time bookies.

Del Fay took in two partners for working capital, each partner paid $10,000.00 each. Now Mike is President and I am Vice President. After the first trip to Vegas a full two hundred and ninety passengers, all bills were paid for and the $10,000.00 cost of the bond is due. There is over forty thousand in the bank. The total costs of the bonds were ten thousand each. On Monday, we had a meeting and Mike who did the bookkeeping. Our profit was $10,000 dollars of which this entire amount went to the Lyell Social Club to pay for all chairs,billiard table and equipment; such as a typewriter and telephone. I was to receive nothing. But I am still responsible for the $30,000 I signed for but that is what is left in the bank.

As I returned home one winter night, I felt like the skinny kid returning home after getting the worst of the fight. Fortunately, we were leaving next day to a conference in Florida with Allstate. Jean and I returned on a Sunday night. As soon as we entered the house I smelled cigarette smoke and knew Mike and our partners must have come over to work on our second charter.

I went down to the basement to look things over. OMG, there were at least a dozen cigarette butts on the floor all paper work was removed and our tote board with passenger information was also gone.

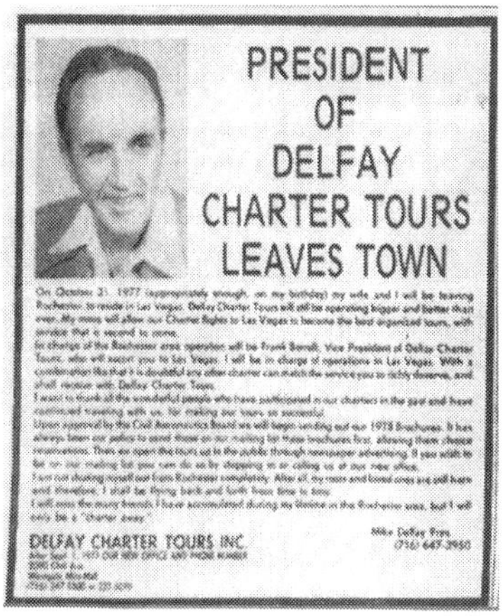
PRESIDENT OF DELFAY CHARTER TOURS LEAVES TOWN

DELFAY CHARTER TOURS INC.

Monday morning, I put in a call to Mike. Now, Mike lived in Vegas. Mike was very cordial when informing me that one of the new partners owned an auto body and fender shop with a large office and staff that would be capable of doing the bookings for the charter flights in the future.

Now enter the post skinny kid from the Green Grass. "Not a problem Mike, I fully understand" "Mike, you know the $30,000 dollars in our checking account, well it is no longer there. "I withdrew the full amount that I signed for to secure bonding." "There is no way you can do that." "Yes, Mike as an officer of the company I am entitled to make withdrawals and deposits as often as I wish." "Well we shall see about this; my nephew Mike Rose will be calling you." I answered, "fantastic Mike, have your lawyer call Lee Ramsey my attorney."

That afternoon I received a call from my friend Lee Ramsey informing me that we have an appointment with another good friend Mike Rose. Understand, that all Italian Americans in Rochester that deal with the public are well known to each other. Another thing that one gets to know is who to mess with and who one must stay away from. At this point I am waiting for my house to explode or my car to blow up.

This is the fast lane that I have learned to stay away from, one in which my little pistols I own, would be nothing in comparison to the artillery that these people can call for.

Wednesday morning, we meet in Mike Rose's office. Both sides of the story are told and there is not a question that I acted legally in taking the money to pay for our commitment on three charters.

It's obvious that we can no longer remain partners so what to do. We agreed to let the lawyers come to an agreement and we will abide by it. There will be more to read about Mike Rose later.

Only me! Leroy and I start for the elevator as we enter Mr. Delfay has us hold the elevator door for a second, so he can join us. Silence, and Mike came through with honor. This I cannot to this day believe, he looks me straight on and says to me "I am only sorry about one thing, you screwed me before I had a chance to screw you." I am not sure; did I win, or did he? If I won, why am I not happy?

The agreement we arrived at was; I will keep the $30,000 to pay for the fiduciary bonds, I will not be responsible for past or future debt. My name will be removed from the corporation and I will have no equity in any past and future profits. Good riddance and **"C'est La Vie."** If only this will be the last time I am taken advantage of. The most upsetting thing is when someone much below your intelligence gets the best of you.

"It ain't over, 'til it's over." I am a glutton for punishment. After the fiasco at the travel agency; there was another disappearance at the agency by another trusted person, the division of the real estate partnership, a water purification company, and finally the profit gained because of selling the duplex in Florida.

Another business started on a ski lift at Holimont. My friend asks me to enter a partnership with Mike Rose, himself and I. Apparently, Dr. Lamar had a college friend that recently came to town and wanted to start a water purifier business that resembled a "Pyramid" scam. Everyone you sign on becomes an independent agency to sell the purifiers. After a while you have a lot of owners but no sales people able to make a living.

1951 to 1954

Jobs were plentiful in 1951. The draft was in force for all those 18 to 35 leaving a lot of jobs not filled. I was going to night school now, taking two subjects on Monday and Wednesday. My first stop was IBM. Great interview and was told that night school was an achievement and if I do complete there will be a job waiting. Next, was Bausch and Lomb, this was a great place the roster of employees was, the majority were German employees. Everyone spoke with an accent. These machinists and instrument makers were the best in the world. I learned how to use various tools used to assemble or manufacturing a total product.

My department made instruments for the medical field and military. This job included Bombsights, Cinemascope lenses. All types of microscopes and other medical and industrial instruments. I met so many great friends and played softball two nights a week in summer. This was a great league and some of these players are in the softball hall of fame. The biggest name there is Harold "shifty" Gears.

This guy could do tricks with his wind up and with his delivery. Unfortunately, the only time I tried to hit him was when he was an umpire for the kids KPAA. I was thirteen and asked if he would pitch one to me. Of course, he took eighty percent of the speed off the pitch. In the winter on Monday and Wednesday nights we played basketball. I had to change my night school to Tuesday and Thursday. This was another time and a different place. I loved every minute of it. Our baseball team was in the "Dusty" League one below the Majors but our pitcher occasionally was Bernie Prince. Bernie pitched for the Majors and was one of the best around. Ritter Dental a large Dental Chair manufacturer, had Frankie Chiacci another Hall of Fame.

All of this was soon to come to an end. In 1952 while "cruising" on a Saturday night with a cute, blond lady; I noticed across the street at the corner of Saratoga and Lyell two girls from the past. No other than Miss Jean and Mary Mitzi, dressed in blue jeans and a sweat shirt on a Saturday Night no less. I hit the horn and gave a wise guy kind of wave; like "Hey, look at me, my new car and look what I have next to me." Little did they know that a few minutes before my guest threw a cigarette butt out of her window, the stupid butt rolled down the window and rested on the ledge of the track. Upon opening the window, the butt followed the glass into the door. I had visions of my new car going up in flames, so I was in a hurry to go to a service station. The pouring of a gallon of water on the window and into the door, solved the problem.

The following day [to this day she will not admit it happened this way] I started receiving calls on the phone at home from all of Jeans friends. All were asking why I was not calling Jean she would love to see you. Jean the same person that after seeing my picture in the paper with a friend, told her mom "guess who died in Korea?" That same Jean almost gave her Mom a heart attack. Her Mom loved the skinny kid from the Green Grass.

I wish I remembered that first call to Jean but obviously, she accepted and I was to call at the house the next day. Now I am no longer the same skinny kid, but a 20-year-old confident adult. I come to 383 Verona Street MR. TESE is on the front porch drinking a Standard Ale. My greeting to MR. TESE was "Hey Carl how are you doing?" No one, but no one ever called Mr. Tese by his first name. But rest assured I called him Dad from the day we were married. **Autres temps autres moeurs**. I was welcomed by Jean's brother, (we graduated together from Jefferson High) and mother and father. The Tacci family, Aunt Anna and Uncle Ignacio [Naiuts] also loved me. These were the four brothers I bragged to, my Army buddies. Wow nine degrees then and finally about twelve. I remember prior to this Aunt Anna invited me to Easter Dinner one Sunday; she loved Frankie.

After two years at B and L, I applied for a job in sales. I wanted to make use of my night school "education." I was refused the job and later found out that my boss Otto Mateush, had too much invested in Frank and could not afford to lose him.

About this time Pat and Nancy asked me, through my connections, to get two watches for a confirmation they were asked to Sponsor. That recalled, that I never got my confirmation watch. Now, I knew from nothing about watches or jewelry. This began the start of my selling jewelry and watch repairs all monies received was used to purchase stock. After a few months people were coming to my home to select to their needs. But I always had the option of consignment.

I walked into Rosenbloom the large wholesaler on St. Paul Street. This was all, new to me, when I arrive there were two doors one had to walk through after you were buzzed in. This place had some expensive stuff inside. When I asked how to go about buying wholesale I was told that first I would have to have a DBA doing business as certificate also a bank account with the business name on it. No problem; first off to the county for a DBA BORRELLI JEWELRY was officially off the ground. Next to Lincoln Alliance Bank and start a checking account with a $10.00 deposit.

Next day back to Rosenbloom and the consignment of six watches with a retail price of $59.00 my cost was $19.00 a watch. Pat picked two and I charged him $30.00 each. They were thrilled, and my checking account now had $32.00 in the account. I now passed the word around Bausch and Lomb and would run out every day to Rosenbloom. Bob was my mentor and taught me how to read his code so, if I brought someone into the store I would know how much my cost is. The code was trade quick "the t is a 1, and R is a 2, ÉTC" until you reach the K and that is O, there are ten letters from one to ten.

At that time, I was in the right age group and sold many engagement rings. Within six months I had at least $5,000.00 in jewelry and watches. Now the bug hits and I start in earnest to gather inventory and purchase some used show cases and cash and wrapping counter. In those days, a one ct. Diamond clear up to a 10-power magnification would sell for maybe $1,200.00 my cost would be $300.00 and sell it for $600.00. Many young lawyers were giving large stones to their fiancées.

Jean and I wasted no time, for Valentine's Day I picked her up at work and while driving down Clinton Ave. I asked her to pick up a card from the rear seat. OMG, when she opened there was a perfect. 75ct. with a .25 on each side in a white gold setting. This stone had a lot of brightness and blueish color she flipped. She then accepted my ring, but next I had to ask her dad and decided on the date of Sept. 7th, Labor Day. So, I was born on Labor Day, enlisted and got discharged on Labor Day. Now married on Labor Day and will have our daughter born on Labor Day.

Wedding went off great and honeymoon to New England to show off where I was stationed went well; then to NYC and Atlantic City. Wrong! Jean got homesick after four days. We are the only newlyweds to return home from a honeymoon with $200.00 in cash. We had to hurry home to our three-room apartment on 82 Locust Street across from Aunt Anna. I could not wait till I went around the Edgerton Grill, our hang out to tell all the guys to come over Saturday for dinner because my wife was a great cook. When I arrived, and gave Jean the news, she almost fainted and wanted to kill me. Jean did not know how to cook. This is the kind of thing that she was later to accept. So, the next day Jean runs to Aunt Anna and pleads her case. Aunt Anna is a great cook and baker.

On Saturday morning along comes Jean and her arms are loaded with veal cutlets, pasta and salad. There was enough food to feed an Army. We kept our secret for a lifetime; this was easy to do because between everyone getting married and moving out of the neighborhood plus having children, your friends are not as often seen.

Married life was great. Quite frankly, we were two young kids age twenty-two and twenty-one and had no idea what was right from wrong. Jean worked for United Utilities; this was a sales organization that had a clientele that bought everything from their salesman that had a territory to cover house to house like the Fuller Brush Sales Agent.

I entered this marriage knowing what I had been was not to continue. No offense to any of our friends that chose to do it differently. My rules would apply period. I had a little help from my in laws. One night after a stupid argument Jean, she decides she is going home to Mother. After getting dressed she informed me that the covers on the bed were given to us as a wedding present from her aunt. I proceed to take them off the bed and she begins walking out of the house before she realizes that we only own one car. Jean proceeds to call her mother to pick her up. After she explains to my mother in law that she wishes to return home. She is told that there is no longer room for her at home so she better be able to work it out. I wish I had a camera, now she returned with all the blankets and proceeded to make the bed, and we lived happily ever after.

After a few months, Jean became pregnant and we must find a larger apartment. Jean's grandfather recently had a fire in his upstairs and remodeled it for us. We had two bedrooms a living room and kitchen. Grandpa Tese lived alone downstairs. Books should be written about him. He was a master builder, plastered and painted Cathedral ceilings. His main accomplishment was the invention of a safe dynamite. While testing for the Army and being accepted someone came up with solid explosive and his was now obsolete. But could "Czatsi" cook; this name of Czatsi somehow in Sicilian slang means grandpa. The aroma from that downstairs was to die for.

Our son Frank, is born in 1954, now it's time for rule number one. The wife will no longer work and will be a full-time mother "period." Now is the time to open the jewelry store from five to nine pm; also, to stop night school and apply to a correspondence school. While at the store I can study, and write exams and homework. I am earning eighty dollars a week at B and L and maybe a hundred at the store. Friends and family also helped as needed. I am also selling mattresses and bedding. One winter afternoon I loaded two box springs and two mattresses on top of the car. I had to delivery on Dewey Ave. While crossing the Smith Street Bridge, the wind blew two of the products off the car. This was in the five o' clock traffic. OMG! The two mattresses were up against the railing; a few more inches and into the river they would go. With the help of a few drivers we attached the mattresses to the top of the car.

Now, not having a choice, B and L was a dead end for me. I applied at the Post Office and as a D.A.V. [disabled veteran] I was put at the top of the list. Every night I would sit with Angelo Marcone, a dear friend, WWII Veteran and Postal Employee. We practiced on old Post Office exams till I was very familiar with the type of exam.

A few weeks later I took the exam, 100 % was the maxim score attainable. Wrong; I got 97% and five points for a veteran, or ten points for a D.A.V. My final mark was a hundred and seven. Within a week, I was a letter carrier. This same month we were awarded a clothing allowance of $300.00 per year. Jackets were the same or like an "Ike Jacket." The following year I had my jacket made into a three-quarter length jacket. There always must be an idiot to do such a thing; but, in the winter my back was very warm; especially when collecting mail from a letter box on some corners. To collect a box the carrier had to bend down exposing your back to the weather.

My jacket extended about ten inches below the waist.

The first assignment was taking a driver's test. The straight or manual shift was very familiar to me so there was no problem. The second week I would be assigned to deliver packages with a Post Office truck. The following week I delivered a set of full size mattress and spring to George Pettrone on Smith Street. I am double parked in front of his house the mattress came out easy but the box spring got stuck in the corner of the truck OMG, what to do now; a passerby stops his car and helps me get it out and comments "Man does the post office ship that large a package and expect you to handle it." You are so right we are over worked.

At the USPO I would start at five am and finish at two. Now I had to hurry home and get to the Jewelry store by three and close at nine. Saturday the hours were noon to six. This was hilarious; my father in law, Cousin Vince, he was studying, (at the U of R Dental School) and Nick Visco would cover till two and I would relieve them dressed in my postal uniform on. Most of our clients knew me personally so it was kosher. My regrets; to this day that I have no photo of our store. Another friend Carm Vullo was a liquor store window designer and every two weeks he did my windows. OMG! They were "Saks Fifth Ave." Just beautiful.

One typical story of my help at the jewelry store must be told. When I relieved my "Compare" Nick at two o'clock' I asked, "how he did" I was told excellent. "I took in $50.00 and sold a ring to Mr. C for $22.00 and he will pay you Monday. That Monday mentioned would have been in 1954. I was never paid that Monday or any other day.

About twenty-five years later my son is waiting in a line at an amusement park. Standing in line behind Frank was a gentleman with his children and a conversation occurred and what is your name? My son answered intelligently, "Frank Borrelli." Great "my name is Mr. C and your dad owes me $22.00 for a ring I purchased from him twenty years ago. OMG! Frankie starts to reach into his pocket to pay him. Then Mr. C suddenly asked and "Do you also know his brother in law? "He is a thief!" At that point, as soon as he spoke bad about Uncle Joe, Frankie put the $20.00 back in his pocket. **"Autres-tempe- autres moires."**

What a joy Frankie has been, soon Jean informs me we are expecting number two child. On September 3 [also Labor Day] Carol Ann is born. Now we go to my second requirement; "as a family we must stick together and be there for each other." There will be no fighting and love must be shown for each other." My third requirement is, that there will be an open house to include our refrigerator for all children's friends. We decide that our apartment is too small. My total pay now is $80.00 from post office and $50.00 from taxi; total amount is $130.00 per week plus my Army disability pension.

We have zero money in the bank and we need to buy a home. The army has a few benefits to former GI's. One is a great guarantee of four and a half percent interest on a mortgage. In either event, we had to have a down payment when we go to a lending institution. I was always good at math, so I figured out that I could borrow the down payment from the Postal Credit Union.

Off we go on our adventure to buy a home. Most homes were priced at $12,000-$14,000. Beach Avenue on the lake was unbelievable at the time. For $15,000, we could have purchased a three bedroom on the lake. Unfortunately, that was out of our league. At that time, there was a huge pollution problem, so I was just as well without. We found a lovely house on Lark Street.

It was a three bedroom, closed porch with a two-car garage for $10,500. I borrowed $2,500 from the Postal Credit Union which had to be paid back for $60.00/month…a piece of cake.

Where ever Mom went "twinkle toes" went.

The day we moved into the home and received our first piece of mail, we received the shock of a lifetime; "after further review of your disability, we are cutting your pension to $19.00 per month. Now, I needed another $100.00 per month to handle expenses. I got a job at Western Auto. It lasted one and a half weeks and I received an example of life as a sales person. My pay was $2.00 per hour and I worked Monday-Friday 5pm-9pm or commission, whichever was greater. $8.00 per night x 3 equals $24.00 per week. My $100.00 per month is a guarantee. The first night of selling I arrived dressed in a suit and tie. I sold two refrigerators, two stoves and one washer. In total, commission was $32.00.

When you consider that Western Auto was a car store but for some reason they tried to sell appliances. On Tuesday night, I arrived prepared to sell. I was told I would stock shelves. Total earnings $8.00. On Friday, I was told to take inventory. Get the picture? If I went home on the first night, I earned $32.00. I worked Wednesday and Friday for zero dollars, I was paid $32.00 for the week. I told the manager, he was a joke, and that I quit.

I was still having fun at the Post Office. Red Triano and I started a baseball league and had twelve teams. We played every Sunday morning. My team was called "Braimans Uniform," a retailer that sold a lot of uniforms to the post office. We thought we had a pretty good team and I booked games against Santillo's (World Champs) slow pitch and I lost $200. I booked a game with Santillos bar patrons next. My father was the pitcher. He was fifty-five at the time. We lost $200.00 again, and it was back to our Sunday morning leagues.

My second year at the Post Office I was elected secretary to the NALC union; I did this for four years. Cab driving was still a fun happening. Never a dull moment; one night I picked up a young 16-year-old with his father and uncle. They came from Toronto to appear at the War Memorial (now called the Blue Cross Arena). I dropped him and his dad off and was told to wait…it was Paul Anca as a 16-year-old. When the father returned to the cab he was wailing "I lost my son." The brother in law immediately said in a Lebanese accent" I should be so lucky! Sixteen years old and already a millionaire he is." At the airport, I was given a five-dollar tip; "not too shabby."

1957-1961

We cannot make ends meet.The loss of most of my GI pension was a killer. While studying through correspondence school was an interim study; it failed to give me the networking I needed.

I lost my job as a cab driver. Either I quit or they let me go? Except; they had more than enough reasons to fire me after I totaled two cabs. But now around 1957, "Hy" Fitch, my dad's boss and the owner of Fitch Furniture called me and offered me a part-time job working on Mondays and Saturdays. This position was to relieve the sales people so they could go home to supper. My hours were five to nine and I would work half day if possible on a Saturday. I made $50.00 per week. My total per month was now up to $630.00. I am still trying to get a sales position full-time.

During this time, we had a full routine. I ate supper home every night and went to the park to picnic at least twice a week.

I never missed a KPAA game of Frankie's; Pop Warner or High School. I always found a way to park my Post Office truck nearby so no one could see me. Frankie never let me know until years later that he saw the truck each time and he knew I was there. Apparently, that meant a lot to him. All is good.

It's unusual how things work. We earned less than most of our friends. All of them earned two paychecks minus babysitter, had extra dress clothing and a second car. My cars were purchased from "Honest John" Collision. I swear that some of these cars drove sideways. Yet, we were the "Pearl Mesta" entertainment. Every weekend our house was the gathering place. We even hired a dance instructor to teach us the "cha cha" and we managed a vacation for many weekends at a cost of $40.00 or $50.00. This I felt, was cheaper than paying a physiatrist.

The time I spent on Lark Street was the best time of my life. Our children made great friends and to this day they are still close. Jean and I had our maid of honor two doors away. On the right side, next door was my younger friend from the green grass. In fact, Cosmo Raimondi lived directly across the street from the green grass which was also three doors away from Al's stand. He was in the "little gang." These kids were about three years younger. Three doors away to our right was, F. Felice, my "compare." I confirmed his son, Richard. This made me his "compare, but to Richard I was his," padrino"; confirmation sponsor. Of course, Richard was given a watch like the one I am still waiting forfrom my "padrino."

The tenth ward which was "uptown" is my old neighborhood. This neighborhood had a heavy Irish and German population. This had to be the cleanest neighborhood in the city. It was also the most slippery in the winter. Frankie and his buddies played street hockey and slid around as if they had ice skates on.

Hello, after work was over at Fitch Furniture at 9:00pm, I am so tired and ready for bed. Wrong. On my way home, I turned onto Lark Street from Bryan Street which was solid ice (thanks kids). I skidded into the curb with my nice new Mercury Cougar. The whole front end had to be replaced. Insurance covered all of it except for $250.00. However, after it was fixed I think it drove sideways.

Frankie and his friends started a band. Where else would they practice? So, I made a club house in our attic. Carol enjoyed her half and moved their fort from the garage to the attic which Frankie and his friends used the rest of the space. They were pretty good. Only my godson Richard, continued and he is the head of the percussion department for Hochstein School of Music in

Rochester.

The positive and negative works both ways; to gain some head room in the attic, it was necessary to bring the side walls close to the center leaving a four-foot crawl space along both walls. The positive was that taller kids had enough head room. The negative was in our move to Ridgeway Avenue, I forgot to take a rendering that I stored in the crawl space. This rendering was to be the only Frank Lloyd Wright house in Rochester. I picked it up next to the curb in front of the house on East Boulevard. This was the size of a large doll house and made to give the original owners a rendering of the finished product. Now, the value my guess is about $50,000. When I called the new owner, I was told it was thrown in the garbage as junk.

Carol had a great group of girls she hung out with. They were a joy and despite the busing between schools, (three high schools and finally back to the original) four different, she made the cheerleading team in her last two. They were great and unfortunately, I paid too much attention to the game and not enough to the cheerleaders.

All was not going well the school system was starting to do things that were not to the kid's best interests. Bussing was started and seniors were affected the most, their team and graduating class was split sometimes between three schools. Both Carol and Frankie were sent to Jefferson. First day of school there was a riot. I drove to school during this madness and picked up Carol and took her to Nazareth Academy. I was told that it was illegal to change schools to avoid the bussing. Who me? No way Sister; I do not live on Lark Street I live on Ridgeway Ave. And then Sister Agnes comes into the room; "Francis I was your English teacher at Aquinas." "Of course, I remember you; you were my favorite teacher." All went well for a year. Except the die is cast!" Our decision was made for us, we owned a lot on Ridgeway but no home was on the lot. A call that night to Fulvio and work was started that week. We have now lived in the same house for the past forty- five years. Both of our children graduated high school and college and married out of our current house on Ridgeway Ave.

Need Picture of Lark St.

Our Lark Street home

This is our current home. It has plenty of land, for the grandchildren to enjoy twelve months a year.

CHAPTER 6

1961 ARRIVAL, THE MAJOR LEAGUES

In Feb. 1961, I reapplied to Allstate Insurance for employment as a Sales Rep. I am sure that I was qualified for the job but after two refusals it is for certain that my friend and compare, Nick Visco had a hand in this, I am forever grateful. OMG finally I was hired at $450.00 per month. (This was $160.00 per month less than my current salary). This was a guarantee and when Ibecome a sales agent, it would be the guarantee or commission whichever was the greater. I had confidence that I would exceed the guarantee.

I resigned from the USPO, and said good bye to all my friends at Fitch. My only recollection was that I wanted to "spit" in Mr. R's face and while all wished me well, one carrier John while shanking my hand said, "I have seen this before, you will be back." My reply to John was "If I were you, I would not bet on it." I also went up and down the aisles looking for "Mr. Gambler" This person saw me receive some cash for a watch I sold and borrowed $20.00. Borrowed is the wrong word he pulled the $20.00 from my hand and asked if he could borrow it. I agreed and watched as he went to the next aisle and made a wager on a sporting event. I am still waiting for the $20.00. Several years later he was promoted to a Station Manager and within a few months was fired for stealing.

A negative regarding my happening with Mr. R, one severe winter my route was a new area in Penfield, this area was awarded house to house delivery. Formerly the patrons would walk to the corner where each homeowner had a small mail box on a rack like structure. Prior to the delivery, I would take out what was called a relay; the carriers would leave the Post Office with a bag full of mail. This would last for a street or two. Afterwards on various corners the carrier would find the next five or six bundles logistically placed for continuing the route. The first two hours of my route was to relay these bundles to the carriers.

While stopped at Winton Rd. and Hillside [the windiest corner in Brighton] a woman heard some vulgarities come from a truck while she was shoveling snow. The time of this occurrence was approximately the time I was delivering the bundles; this was also the time two other postal trucks were in the area, one Parcel Post and one other relay man. When I returned, Mr. R confronted me with this beauty; "A 72-year-old woman called and said that you opened the door to the truck swore at her and slammed the door shut." "I never would do such a thing like that to an elderly woman, also, I drive with my sliding door open all day, if I were to shut the door it would freeze shut and I would not be able to open it again." His reply was "she was bending over shoveling so you would not be able to know if she were young or old. I told him not to say another word and as Secretary to the Union, I wanted Bernie Murphy the President of the Union present. His last remark sent me over the edge. "As a supervisor, I know that these carriers are capable of doing this kind of thing." Sir I am sorry, but I have more respect for my fellow carriers to think of any one of them doing such a thing; if I did not believe that, I would quit tomorrow. Furthermore, I want this resolved today I am not waiting for the weekend." Later that day Mr. confronted the two other drivers that were in Brighton that same time. His approach was the same way accusing rather than inquiring.

I was unable to sleep all weekend. But I knew for sure that if Allstate came through I am out of there. Eureka about two am. on Sunday. I awaken with the whole scene plain as day. To gain entrance to the storage box on the corner I had to go over a four-foot mound of plowed snow, my truck was about three feet away from the curb because of the large amount of snow. A large Monroe tree surgeons truck with a "cherry picker" on top sped by and had to curve over to the left. Having conventional doors, the passenger could open the door and shout at me. You so and so you are blocking the lane. He then slammed the door shut. This was documented and placed on Mr. R's desk with no comments, the day I received my acceptance from Allstate.

Two years later when I was fortunate to have the travel agency and Allstate Insurance in the Lincoln Tower, Mr. R was on Jury Duty and was excused for lunch. During his break, he strolled into the Travel Agency while I was talking to Georgie, I turned and saw him and man I am all decked out in my Hickey Freeman suit and cuff link shirt. Already looked in my magic mirror and felt like a six foot, millionaire business man. He says, "Hello Frank how are you; want to do lunch?" "That's all she wrote." Mr. R., I had no use for you, when I left the Post Office and I sure as hell have no use for you now, please leave this office." Not a very nice thing to do, not Christian; but the boys on the green grass would approve of what I did. Mea Culpa, Mea Maxima Culpa!

Allstate sent me to school at Jamestown Community College, to study under the Winchester Brothers. These two brothers were the best in getting a high percentage of students their license.

During this month, Allstate opened a large office on Monroe Ave. There was to be over six hundred employees here and a state of the art computer room. This room was dust proof and vibration proof. Employees wore white hats and sanitary gowns. This was the beginning of the Computer age. **"Autres temps, autres moeurs."** Both Jean and I were invited to the grand opening. We were greeted very warmly and got to meet the top producers Dick Skuse and Bert Faraone.

Now, I am twenty-nine, and did not have ten cents in the bank, and have gone two months with a deficit pay of $200.00 per month. As we leave the party, Jean asks me what I thought of the job and if I felt I could compete at this level? My reply was off the charts and typical of one of the "boys from the green grass." "Not a problem, all I must do is outsell those two guys, Dick and Bert. A piece of cake." No doubt in my mind that I will respect both and beat the hell out of them. I became great friends with both and was in awe of Bert Faraone. I out sold both, and I tried to emulate on Bert he was a class guy. Dick was younger than Bert and more competitive but both he and his family became my bench mark. Both Dick and Ginny took us under their wing and our families shared all the conferences together. Their children were as mischievous as ours and it was fun. Ginny was so smart in the Arts and was great to smooth some of my edges. Ginny even knew the name of Little Boy Blue's dog; Wonder. How about that from a kid that came from the green grass?

For the next twenty years, I out sold Bert and went toe to toe with Dick. I truly became the bench mark to beat. At times management used me as a pawn to increase sales. Once Tom Condon our sales manager asked if I thought I could write a hundred applications in one month. This has never been done up to that time. There were a few days left in that month so we agreed to start at the first of the month.

If I wrote the hundred applications, I would get a tailor-made suit from Timely Clothes. Timely, was second only to Hickey Freeman; and my measurements were put on file. I wrote one hundred and seven for the month. I received the first free suite and purchased another. I was now hooked on custom made and never purchased unless tailored; I would buy at the factory outlets. Years later when I meet Adriano Roberti owner of Adrian Jules; he became my Custom Tailor. I also only wore tailored made shirts with French cuffs.

A secret never told before; for the next eight or ten days, every application that I wrote, unless it had to be dated prior to the first of the month was "sand bagged" and dated after the first. Because of my little kitty, I only needed eighty-eight applications to hit a hundred. So now I am a hero! And the 100-Application Club was formed.

The next month no one except one makes the club. Give the man a new suit. Three months later again there is only one winner. The club was disbanded the next month for lack of participation. My new ward robe now contained six custom made suits; three free and three purchased at wholesale. Not too shabby for a kid from the green grass. Tom Condon was transferred or left the company and the club was disbanded. I was hooked; six tailored made suits and several cuff link shirts, sharp ties and nothing different will be worn by me. Some days I had to change into a clean fresh shirt for evening calls. Enter my friend Adriano Roberti; owner of Andrian Jules tailor made suits.

My family has such fond memories of all the conferences and incentives to wonderful places like New York, San Francisco and Hollywood, Mexico Olympics in 1968, Europe and Hawaii, Puerto Rico and so many other destinations. The planning for these conferences was done by Marvin Himmel of Chicago. This person and his team were flawless. What I learned from him I brought back to the little ole travel agency. This education cannot be taught in any class. There were no travel agencies doing any corporate incentive travel that can come close to this agency from Chicago.

I tried to copy on Marv. The greatest was when on some of these trips Frankie and Carol came along. The kids met children of other families. They all were mischievous and needed no coaxing.

In 1961, there was a rule. If you could make the Conference of Champions for ten consecutive years you would become a "life time member" meaning you will be invited every year if you succeeded in writing the minimum production required by the company {a piece of cake} especially for what you gained. Also, to qualify you had to start as an agent prior to June 1st of your first year. I started as an Agent on June 6, 1961. That year I out- sold all agents that started on June 1st or prior. I also outsold all the "High Rollers."

This was not an issue because I knew I could, and did make the conference twenty-two years in a row. Hello! In my tenth year, they stopped the program altogether. I wonder why? Could it be that the only person to qualify that year would have been the skinny kid from the Green Grass? This was my mind set at that time. Maybe a persecuted kind of feeling came easily for many Italian Americans. Regardless what my status was at that time, I was always at the top of my group from rookie to Senior Account Agent.

Frank J. Borrelli Jr. has received a Gold Medal Award from Allstate Life Insurance Co., according to regional manager Herbert E. Lister.

Borrelli was one of three Allstate salesman to receive the award among a force of more than 8,000. It is emblematic of extraordinary sales.

Frank Borrelli has been named winner of the Allstate Insurance Cos. 'Silver VIP Health Award. Borrelli was in the top 1 per cent of Allstate health

Frank J. Borrelli has been promoted to account agent by Allstate Insurance Cos., according to Jack O'Loughlin, regional manager. Borrelli joined Allstate in 1961 and has been an agent in the Allstate office at 259 Monroe Ave. He will now work at the Allstate Insurance Center, 14 Main St. W.

On Tap: An Exciting Ceremony

"Well, it's about that time," said Frank Borrelli to Jean as the band struck up the intro music.

Circa 1965

Conference Circa 1964

Frank J. Borrelli Jr., 237 Lark St., recently attended the Allstate Life Insurance conference in Mexico City. Borrelli is an agent at Allstate's 14 Main St. W. office.

Of the hundreds of awards and accolades I received in my forty years at Allstate, none were more meaningful than those in which I was sought out to present or discuss topics of importance to the company. I cannot give a reason why I needed this, but I really thrived on the attention.

Some of the examples were:

- **26 Conference of Champions** *(always at a great resort; once to the Olympics)*
- **Number one or two in the region for at least twenty-six years**
- **Hundreds of articles in the paper**
- **Dozens of trophies**
- **Average of two fun trips a year**

Most of my friends and relatives would call this being "cocky" or a braggart, but we had a saying in the Army, "don't talk the talk unless you have walked the walk."

For some reason, I had to have attention, so it was extremely important to achieve numbers, that meant having to "kick ass."

I think this attitude came from a desire to have what I did not have when I was a kid.

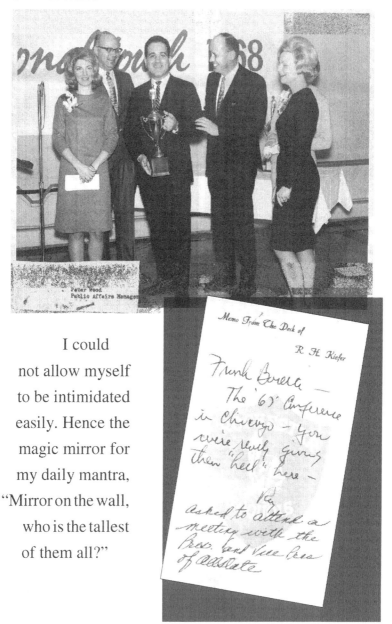

I could not allow myself to be intimidated easily. Hence the magic mirror for my daily mantra, "Mirror on the wall, who is the tallest of them all?"

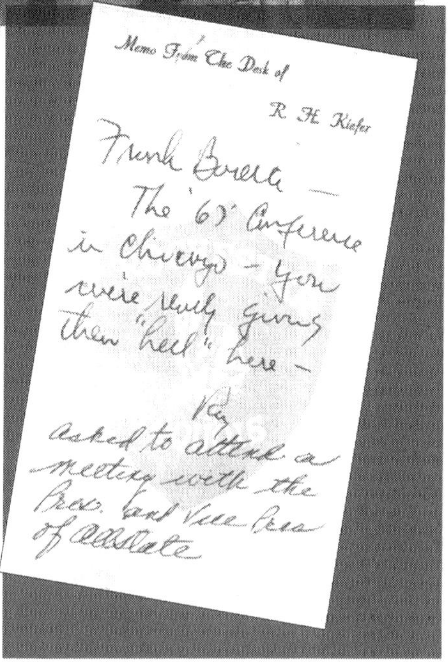
Memo From The Desk of

R. H. Kiefer

Frank Borelli —
The '65' Conference
in Chicago – you
were really giving
them "hell" here –

Ray

asked to attend a
meeting with the
Pres. and Vice Pres
of Allstate

In 1970 Mel Passman, a life member put out his numbers for the year. He was named the Senior Account agent of the year. That year I out preformed Mel in every category. I immediately got up from my chair and while walking to the door threw the "trinket' pocket knife [this was engraved with an Iroquois Indian, our region's logo] at the Sales Manager and walked away from the meeting room. While exiting the building; the Sales manager came up to me and gave me back the knife. I said some nasty words to him that I regret now. I was then and remained thinned skin.

1968.... I never had a boat in my life so...my first one end up a 28' Cabin Cruiser, that I never learned to dock. My 14-year-old son had to dock it for me.

At one of the Conference of Champions I went as number two. I failed to walk through the Honor Ring {an eight-foot replica of a ring]. While seated with Mr. and Mrs. Passman; out of the blue Mrs. Passman asked me "How does it feel to fall flat on your face? We all have been waiting for it to happen?" "After all you came here as the youngest and good-looking couple." OMG, are you for real? I am here maybe number two out of three hundred agents and I should complain...All this free!

After this and dozens of things less than honorable, I felt I was just a number and the day I would leave Allstate, I could call back and identify myself and for a response hear "Frank who?" I was just a number and "would cry all the way to the bank."

During these first ten years with Allstate, I still had that chip on my shoulder. I was obsessed with being on top. I started to make money and always wanted to protect myself. Intelligence was so important to me. I began to hang with my great friend from Montrose St. two doors away. Lee Ramsey, an attorney was the same age and a kid from a divorce from maybe age twelve. Lee's father was from Virginia and his mom was a professional waitress [She worked with my mother at the large first-class restaurants down town]. Lee introduced me to skiing and the law and dental community in Rochester. I enjoyed having lunch with a lot of the lawyers and at night the dental community with Jean's cousin Vincent Tacci, DDS.

THE LAND OWNER AKA PROPERTY RICH AND MONEY POOR

The five properties with Fulvio and Angelo gave me some insight on how to wheel and deal. I am not going into the "would of, could of, and should have" of which there are these in all our lives. I tend to this day to dwell on the past and ask myself why did I do or not do so many things. I no longer have the magic mirror; if I did I think it would tell me that with all my skills and assets being what they are; I accomplished as much or more than could be expected.

The GI bill on education was running out but in those days' large employers would reimburse you for tuition. My last course was during summer school at the University of Rochester. It was political science; the professor was from India. This was about 1965 and I enjoyed every bit of it. It was definitely, Autres temps-Autres moeurs. The professor smoked his pipe at the front desk and spoke through clenched teeth. He was a great teacher. One thing I remember vividly; the year was 1965 and he said to the class "our country is wrong in trying to force a Democracy on all countries. Some countries cannot ever survive in a Democracy.

Nor will they ever be a self-sufficient society." How true this is today and we lost so many beautiful young kids trying.

The able body young men of these countries, will not fight for their own countries. This saddens me because I witnessed some of this mentality.

In 1969 after going to all the Ski Schools in Canada we all figured we were good. We all joined Holimont ski club. Now after age seventy all benefits are free: once again not too shabby. This is great but how many years can you still ski after seventy-five. Now that I am eighty-five both Jean and I walk around the place with our photo membership card around our neck. Unfortunately, all future skiing will be done in the next lifetime.

Ain't she Pu-rity?

During our first year at Holimont, we all rented a motel suite in Olean every Fri and Sat. from Oct. to April. This was a 22-mile trek but it was wonderful to be with Frank and Carol. We watched as they started in the class with other kids their age in learning how to "snow plow." Next came the "moguls" or mounds of snow. They were skiing like pros, well maybe not that good but to us they were outstanding.

Our ski trailer, notice the spacious front and side.

We had a group of five families. All families had at least two or three children. The second year it was decided that we would all buy trailers and place them in a trailer park.

Two were lawyers, one dentist, one self-employed and the Borrelli's. Someone with a lot of time had to go to Olean and negotiate with the trailer park and the trailer seller. Guess who? Yep, the kid from the Green Grass went to the trailer sales in Olean to begin to work on a deal. "Hello, I am here to make a deal; I want to purchase four trailers loaded, also one with no furniture at all and a wee bit smaller." I reached a deal $9,500.00 dollars for the big ones and $4,500.00 for the smaller one ... Deal! "Dad I need two bedrooms of furniture one with bunk beds. Also, one kitchen set and living room set with end tables and lamps. Dad had connections like no one I ever knew.

The Amerks Hockey Club was another deal. We never paid to get in, because his friend "Hardy" from the old neighborhood was the ticket taker. Hardy also got all kinds of autographed sticks for Frankie. The best of all, at half time a ticket number is called and that person get to shoot from center ice at the goal. Some of the opening is blocked off and replaced with a one foot wide opening. The winner gets twenty-five gallons of gasoline at the service station that was an advertiser. Frankie was eleven years old and his number was called for three straight weeks. The best he did was barely reach the hole but stopped directly in front of the hole. Paul Napier was the announcer and sat next to the gate that we went through to enter the ice. I knew Paul from Aquinas. As we returned from the ice Paul started with the "I thought it was you, how in the heck did you pull this off?" Frankie got wise and refused to go on the ice another time.

My Dad worked at a large furniture store. Dad oversaw all the touch up men; these were furniture refinishers and the union delivery drivers were under him also. Dad managed to find all the scratched furniture. What was not scratched he helped it along. Next to the store manager and ask how much for all that damaged "as is" furniture for Junior. On average about $10.00 per item not too shabby! Next, he took it all to the "Swede"; he told Swede to fix and polish like new for Junior. I still have some tables at the ski house.

These were the best five years of our lives. We did not miss one week of skiing. Every week we would meet half way at a small restaurant in Corfu a small town before Arcade NY, about 45 miles from our home. Ellicottville is ninety-five miles from Rochester so we were half way. We were five couples with ten children and the time was five pm. We would eat up a storm and proceed to the trailers with bags of groceries for the week end. Frankie had his college friends over during the week I would think. Bonaventure was only twenty miles away. On his graduation, we had a party in town and at the trailer. Those New York City and Philly Boys were so much fun. We were at least twenty people in a 10 x 50 trailer.

I was unable to keep my father away from the fresh clams that Chirmonti's Dad brought from his favorite spot on Long Island. Dad never bragged about clams again unless he told the story of the Long Islander.

1970 TO 2014 TRAVEL AGENCY

Our little travel agency captured some big-time conferences and yearly groups. Many groups I put together and escorted in much the same manner as Marvin; we ran over a hundred trips of forty or more to Europe; I loved it. At least one trips a year skiing. Usually I would go all alone and scout out the hotels to be used in Italy, Austria or Switzerland. One time, Jean came with me and it was Octoberfest; wow what an experience. We were on the Autobahn where there is no speed limit. My small Fiat that I rented allowed me to stay the heck out of the way and just let everyone pass.

Not too shabby for a novice business owner.

Another group I enjoyed was the anesthesiologists four-thousand strong in December of every year for twenty years. To accommodate these folks, I entered into agreements with four of the top hotels in New York City. We saved the largest for the headquarters of the organization and a desk up front for my staff.

Our allotment of rooms always included at least four "comp-rooms." We peaked out at eleven employees and two outside sales people.

The start of the travel was a piece of work. This was the first year of Airline Automation. We did not have customer one; I had a few years of selling travel to mostly first-generation Italian and European clients.

My x-partner and Clara our Italian/English teacher could communicate. All reservations were made via a phone call to a travel agency desk at the airline you chose. There was a book or manual called the OAG, which we subscribed to. This gave you the airlines that serviced all national and international destinations. But, to compare prices we would have to call each airline individually. This was archaic to say the least.

"Autres temps, autres moeurs."

To qualify for a computer system at that time, an agency should have at least $2,000,000 in volume. We didn't even have bookings yet, upon looking back at this I must have been crazy.

After I ordered the automation I realized we had to be able to type. (I think now it's called keyboarding). Signora could type one-hundred words an even then at least eight-five word per minute. Now is the clincher; Ann was our super sales person, but knew nothing about the various destinations, she could read brochures and destination pamphlets to get info. Next, I am informed "Dad I do not know how to type". OMG what to do now? "Ann here's the plan, go across the street to Bryant and Stratton a clerical school and enroll. [Ann now has a four-year-old granddaughter that can type] a different time.

Jean and I flew to Dallas, Texas and enrolled for a two-week course at American Airline's training center. Ann was left to fend for herself. I have no idea how, but she sold a woman that oversaw travel for the female Olympic athletes. For the next four years, we did the travel for the women on the Olympics. This also included all travel that they did when they boycotted the Russian games. They went to the Pan Am games instead.

Along about this time I receive a call from Ann; "Dad I have a girl here that you have to hire. She is the smartest person I have met and speaks various languages including French." I don't think we ever wrote a ticket to France. But Kathee just graduated from the Sorbonne in France. Kathee not only was the brightest person but she was my clone. Her birthday was also Sept. 7th; two Virgos in the same office and you have oil and water. OMG, it was scary but she not only could sell but she was able to bond with all our clients. Kathee had the ability to walk into an office in our building and capture their business because of her preparation and knowledge of the business.

Before going out on a call she researched the company and I am sure she said what they wanted to hear.

After a few years, Signora got tired of the "snippy" secretaries and retired. By the end of our first year because of Ann and Kathee we grew to six employees and were doing over one million dollars in corporate travel. We ultimately grew to about five million. Once Kathee matured I knew she out grew this job.

By this time, I knew all the sales reps of American Airlines, United, US Air and all the international carriers. We started with a US Air computer system but later went to the bench mark; the Sabre System owned by American Airlines. Sabre was breaking away from American and opened a large training school in Tampa. They were looking for instructors; and I knew this was a natural for Kathee.

I called Tampa and spoke to the titled person whose name I have forgotten. I asked if they needed any great help. I was told that they were looking for instructors. My remark to him was; "I don't think you understand, this person after one week will be able to teach your instructors." I think I jarred him out of his undies. He sort of took this as a dare to put up or shut up. I mentioned all this to Kathee and was sad and bored now that I had no one to challenge me daily. We promised to continue to celebrate our common birthday.

Guess what happened! Of course, she could not teach the instructors in two weeks, it took her one month and she was running the operation. Maybe I am embellishing it a wee bit but she put in twenty fabulous years as a leader at American Airlines.

The business may have been started by me with the help of Ann and Jean and a fabulous location of that era. Downtown Rochester was a hustle and bustle active area then. I worked at Allstate all day and could stop in for an hour or two. I hired Ange from his retirement from the post office. Very honest and he handled all our weekly reports. To assist Ange with the computer reports we had Barbara and a few part time people. We had Jane Murray and another woman always to assist with Leisure Travel. Before the development of total computer reservations, we delivered tickets and itinerary to the client's office or home. We owned a new pickup truck and hired a young person and paid for their education, at night school.

We were growing, we had an office in the Detroit home office of Chrysler also Schelgel Corporation in Rochester. Jane V. was in charge of this operation. She was so well entrenched that she quit and went elsewhere and took the accounts with her as an incentive for her new position. Next, we had a new hire in our leisure dept. She took a cash sale and purchased a new wardrobe. This sale amounted to over a thousand dollars. I called the client and told her that I had "misplaced her check." I was told she was traveling with a well-known personality and he paid cash so there would be no audit trail of his travel with her. I told her that all was well, I failed to look at the cash sales.

I then fired the person; fortunately, her mother worked at a police department. I gave the mother two options the money within the hour or I call the police. I was paid in full in thirty minutes.

The last of the negatives was at Christmas day 1976. I received a call from a woman that I watched grow from an infant to a married mother of two children. Her father was also a member of the green grass gang. This person started working for a rival travel agency. Ms. untrustworthy was a great sales person and would do anything to make the sale (this regardless what it took attitude was unknown to me). I recommended to her to go it alone and place the business through an agency and earn a commission. From day one she exceeded any pay received as an agent. Fantastic, I gave her a desk in a branch office I opened at 4210 West Ridge Rd. at no cost. Occasionally Ms. untrustworthy would answer the phone and turn the call over to our employee that was full time.

An owner of a dental laboratory was referred to BTS by a dentist friend. BTS never heard from this person. Mrs. untrustworthy took the call, and did their reservation as she would her client. On Christmas Day, I received a call that Ms. untrustworthy claiming that she had a bunch of tickets due on Christmas, all first class to Europe. The total was to be paid by credit card, over $15,000 dollars. As if I knew! My advice was, under no condition are you to play any games be sure to check with the airlines. Be extremely cautious because it is a holiday and airlines may be short staffed. Mr. Rodrigues's credit card was declined three times yet Ms. untrustworthy forged an approval number. Weeks later, I was asked to pay the airlines for this mistake. I paid and took her to a hearing and won. I proved she was not an employee but an independent contractor. I did not pursue any recourse and failed to go after her in a civil case for. I was so upset that I could not think straight. I could have had her arrested if I turned in a "subcontractor dishonesty" claim.

Families and many friends were lost because of this act of dishonesty. But I was riding high on finances and bit the bullet.

OMG, three months later, I received a call from Eastern Airlines. Eastern went out of business two months prior. I was told that my company wrote dozens of tickets for less than half the regular price to Puerto Rico. I must now pay approximately $12,000.00 or fly to New York City for a hearing. I hired a lawyer that convinced them that it would not be in their best interest to come from Miami to have a trial. We settled for $8,000.00. Total amount of my loss was over $20,000.00 plus legal fees and the loss of many longtime friends. This is another C'est la vies!

Those are the main negatives, as per my beliefs the positives must come. We had the best of the best not only were we one of the top agencies and had the best travel agents but they had great "people skills." When I sold the agency, we had five people that were with me for twenty years or more. I feel I must now give credit for the best staff in the industry. They were all so good that they taught this material at St John Fisher College. What an honor for the skinny kid to have been offered to "chair" the new travel and tourist class at St. John Fisher College. [I delivered mail to the college, their first Christmas and a few months after. This was about 1956 while a post office substitute]. I helped the regular letter carrier.

With the addition of Kathee we now had three employees. Along came a young lady Karen shortly after came Patricia, Jane, Loraine, Patty, Michael, George, Carol, Paula and Barbara. This is the bulk of the people that made us one of the most respected Agency's in the system. Daily, we dealt with some of the top companies in Rochester; including the United States Olympics. There were dozens more I could name but these were really the bulwark that I was proudest of. Some of the other "wannabees" did not have longevity; especially when they realized it was hard work and travel agents do not travel as much as some folks thought. But I will say the above-mentioned group was in the business when we took many "fam trips" familiar trips to all parts of the world.

All the above names and dozens more I loved them all. I could work full time including night time house calls and conferences and knew the business was in good hands, no pun intended. I worked for the Good Hands people at Allstate Insurance. Allstate employees were not allowed to "moon light" or have a business on the side. Fortunately, our DBA was Jean Borrelli a woman owned business. A jealous anonymous caller once called management at Allstate and the skinny kid was called into regional Headquarters in Chicago. OMG, they were messing with a woman owned business how dare they? That ends that story for the next thirty years. The last words to me were just; keep up the good work selling.

Now Karen; Bella Karen; "membro della mia famiglia" (a member of my family). Karen came to Rochester as a recent college graduate and started to work at Liberty Travel. The potential was there to do better than work on "Honeymoon packages." Karen Lisi grew up in Corning, N.Y. When Karen applied, she was about twenty-one and we got to know her mom and dad and family. Karen lived alone had no relatives here so we were her family. First came the wedding to Dana. We helped secure a date with a golf club that was managed by a friend from the post office. All seemed to go according to plan. What some fun weddings we had. Karen's lovely Mom had a great time I remember her dancing. That was the last I saw of Mrs. Lisi; shortly after she passed away. I remember going to Corning with a load of Italian food like all of us from the Green Grass were taught.

Karen came back to work and never left her desk up to this date. Well not really but she has not taken a lunch break in twenty-five years. I have never seen anything like it. She has natural people skills; all her clients will talk to only Karen. I have heard her battle airlines or a tour operator to get every bit of service the client has coming to them.

Karen could do all our weekly reports at week's end. All accounting was also done daily before we could afford a bookkeeper. Every group she had a hand in it. For about twelve years we did the NYS Society of Anesthesiologists. This was big we hit the big time with this over four thousand rooms and at least seven thousand Doctors. We also had to find rooms for the hundreds of vendors that paid for display space in the hotels. We dealt with Hilton, Hyatt, Sheraton and Marriott and several smaller hotels. These rates had to be negotiated. Entertainment and activities was handled by the association in NYC. We staffed a desk in the lobby and made sure all was taken care of with the room selection including the comp rooms and the floors that have access to the VIP lounge.

The typical thing that I would have to solve. (keep in mind most Eastern European doctors did not have credit cards). Their trip was usually paid for by pharmaceutical companies. A lovely couple came to our desk. Their entire luggage was lost by the airlines. This couple was staying at a hotel that was very inexpensive and not one of ours. The wife spoke no English only Polish. Many tears were shed. First, I bought them dinner. Next there were no rooms anywhere so off to the YMCA we went. This lovely couple was dressed as any of us would for a seven-hour flight; Levi's and sweater. I think they wanted to kiss my ring as if I was the Pope. The following day a prince and her knight came to our desk to model how they were dressed. You guessed it, here was the Raggedy Ann couple from Poland all decked out and we were their first stop. They wanted to show us that they also belonged as a part of this group. They really were a cute couple and so appreciative for what I did. **C'ie le vie.**

Karen also helped in formatting along with Kathee our course material for St. John Fisher College Travel Program. Our startup was at the travel agency using only the front area. There were three distinct sections. Our front reception and leisure department was large enough for about twelve students. At the college in our third year we once had thirty students.

About this time while at the Chase Lincoln Tower; our agency was in the Concourse of Shops. Across the hall there was a barber shop owned by Louis Benini [Lou cut Mr. Arnold B. Swift's hair]. Mr. Swift was the former principal of Jefferson High. Mr. Swift in my estimation was the greatest educator I have ever met. Next to Lou, there was a sporting goods store a Tennis Pro Shop. Frank Ciacci a big time fast pitcher was the owner. Frank was on a par with Shifty Gears. Frank is also in the hall of fame. The shop was the only one in the country allowed to use the name of Head Racquets; the shop was called "Competition One"; named after Head's most popular racquet. I don't know how he pulled this off.

Frank had the finest of clothes and racquets and had a knowledgeable woman Jane as a stringer and sales person. The sport shop came up for sale and Frankie my son "always wanted to own a sport shop." This was a tennis shop not baseball or football shop; never the less I purchased the shop. What a great education this was. We did not lose money, but there were little profits. The line of clothes we sold was top of the line. We carried the best racquets Prince, Head, Wilson and a few others. We also strung about five to ten rackets a day. We had a Dunlap stringer that was the best of its time. After two years Penfield sports bought us out. Whatever the cost, he left the day after Christmas. He stripped the inventory to the wall and left town owing us a great deal of money. Of course, we went to court but somehow, he claimed he was bankrupt. You win a few and lose a few. **"C'ie la vie."**

Gone are the days of the Charters to Vegas. Those were fun and a different type of education. Not being a gambler and seeing gamblers all my life was a turn off for me but it was exciting. After a few years, you are treated like a native. Most people are phonies in those places and when a local meets a "straight" person, they celebrate and call all their friends to meet the straight person. When in Vegas if in doubt just tell them that "Butch sent you," trust me there always is a Butch person somewhere in the Casino.

After five years, we sold the trailers. Leroy quit skiing. The clown Prince Sam also quit the club and went to Florida. Frank Casacelli also quit the club. Dr. Lamar sold and bought a new town house one of a new development with over fifty units. Five years later Dr. Lamar quit the club.

Losing my entire group of friends at the club I was tempted to quit. While going to the lodge to quit; I noticed a newly converted double at the bottom of the hill for about $90,000.00. Our home is two hundred feet to the Meadow Chair. We since have added two additions. We now have; eight bedrooms two kitchens and five bathrooms. This has been my dream of a lifetime a close family [the closer the better] and a place for all of them and their families. It has been awesome Christmas week and New Year's it's theirs and their friends. Never in twenty years has any one of my kids or grandkids abused the privilege. In fact, when these kids and friends leave, the place is as clean as when they arrived. I am so proud and for some reason they still ask occasionally if they can have a friend over for a weekend. All my friends that sold, I wonder if they regret continuing at the club. Different strokes for different folks. I think it can also be described as Autre temps-autre moeurs.

I am so happy that now, the "ski Haus" and the two places in Florida are being enjoyed by all these kids and their friends. My great grandson Noah hears anyone mention the" ski Haus," or Ellicottville and he gets so excited. Two years old and he gets the picture, I bet he will be on skis by three.

There was a British Field Marshall in Europe in World War II. Any time Field Marshall Montgomery gave an order he immediately had a plan on what to do when and not if the person screwed up. He was as sure as an "axiom" that the person would screw up. This is the same as I feel about partnerships. After a while partners begin to feel like martyrs; each partner feels that they are 100% right in feeling that they do more than their share of the work.

On Lake Ave, we had a great thing going; I almost bought the Trailer Park in Ellicottville. I had the check book in my pocket the name of our company was Fell-Bor. Very original Felice and Borrelli. With Ange and I not knowing much about building we had more laughs. Ange was left handed and more of a desk worker but we managed to fix our mistakes with" Plastic Wood" filler. Had I put the ten thousand down on the Trailer park with a purchase of fifty-eight thousand they would not have said a thing. Our lawyer my dear friend Lee Ramsey, told me not to buy because the state would force us to put sewers in and this would involve digging under the stream that passed through the Park.

Some Canadian purchased it for the ninety-eight thousand and the State did force the sewer thing. But the State ran the lines from the town to the Park free. Upon completion, he sold all the land and the park for one million dollars. C'est la vie. If the three of us had to do it over we would. I am sure that my Compare Fulvio and Ange are agreeing with me now from Heaven. We had such a great time and more laughs than anyone can imagine, plus we made money when we sold.

Associations and acquaintances are not always true friends. I have found that my only true friends are those friends from school days. My friends from the green grass after marriage lost all touch with each other. Brown square kids to this day meet twice a month for lunch. From a gang of sixty or seventy guys; only one person purchased insurance from me. Billy Benedict the only non-Italian in the gang gave me all his family insurance. The Brown Square gang gave me at least thirty policies. Apparently, we had a lot of envious kids among those that hung out at the green grass. C'est la vie, Nick Visco is more than a true friend; he is my brother. I am convinced now to avoid any joint ventures.

1980 TO 1998: FROM THE BEGINNING

Well almost!! Now, Allstate came up with a great plan. If a qualified agent wanted to purchase a property and open an Allstate Office, money would be provided for a down payment and money for remodeling. Now I am on a mission, I find a location at Latta and Long Pond Rd. This was an old bank building. I let it go because of the amount to change from a bank to a mercantile would be too expensive and the loss of space for the built in safe would also be a negative.

Finally, I find a great building at 4210 West Ridge Rd. The building had six great pillars in front that reminded me of an ante bellum home. I figured an Allstate office on the right side and a Borrelli Travel Branch on the left and a realtor upstairs. Price for this house [from Eastman Kodak formerly to house transient employees] was eighty thousand. Allstate would give me forty thousand, plus six hundred dollars for rent per month.

First person and hopefully the only one I called was Nick Visco. Nick also loves everyone and never creates waves. Nick wants to ask John, Bob, Gerry and Jack to join us. So much said for my new methods! Jack really does not want to go in business with a bunch of Italians. Great that is one less!

Our down payment on this purchase was only twenty-five hundred. I agreed on the four extras. The next day I receive a call from a lawyer representing Gerry and wanting to know my history and what protection Gerry would have if he invested with us. The lawyer wants to be sure his client was not "short changed." Outstanding, I hung up and called Gerry to inform him that I no longer want him in the equation. Gerry now had a choice to go it alone or pay rent to the remaining four. I learned something in the Army and Sgt. Borrelli has taken a stand.

I ran the meeting and informed John and Bob that I really did not want them involved, but Nick is your friend and for Nick I am allowing you two in. [I referred John to Allstate from his truck driving job about eight years prior]. I am allowing you in with one stipulation; when we sell, you will each pay Nick and me five thousand each regardless of the proceeds. Nick felt it might be a little stiff. My response to all was that if Nick did not want his five thousand, I would then take the full ten thousand. Nick agreed!

We sold five years later for two hundred and twenty-five thousand. It seemed later at the sale, both John and Bob seemed to forget the rules. "After all we are all friends now etc." After I reminded them of the agreement Bob recalled and told John that an agreement was in place. Both Nick and I received five thousand each over and above the equal split.

After a few years, a large parcel of land next door came up for sale, twelve acres for fifty thousand. I purchased and asked Nick if he wanted half of the action. He agreed and wanted Sam Lipari also to be asked, I agreed and wanted Cousin Vince also. We bought the five acres of land for twelve thousand five hundred each, and held the land for a few years. About four years later, Sam has a buyer for two hundred thousand so, our twelve thousand five-hundred-dollar investment returned to us fifty thousand each. It seems I will never learn about "splitting the pie." Well almost never but one more time I promise.

In 1995, I received a call from Rocco DiStaffen asking if I would like to go into partners with him and my son Frankie. I agreed and Rocco asked me how much he should offer for the building a former pizza place? I informed Rocco that he should not hesitate to offer the asking price. Little did I know this house was a disaster waiting to happen? Rat infestation and droppings and holes all over the place; the asking price was one hundred twenty-five thousand dollars. Apparently, the listing expired with no sale the week before. Prior asking price was ninety-five thousand and he would have accepted eighty thousand dollars.

Apparently, the week before the real estate agent was acting as an agent and now he was acting as a broker and built in whatever he felt he wanted to make on the sale. Taking my grievance to the Real Estate Board was a waste of time. The realtor's comment was "apparently, Mr. Borrelli and Son now find that they cannot afford what they purchased and are desperate." C'est la vie. To me he was a thief and will always be a small-time operator. He later sold his business and just faded away.

After a year, the four-family house next door became for sale. This front yard gave us much needed parking space, and a little additional rent income for me. When I retired, and moved our main office of the Travel Agency in a shared location with Frankie, I sold both my share of Allstate and the four family to Rocky at cost.

Enough already; from here I go it alone. Frank Davis was a client of Borrelli Travel and a great friend. He was opening a large B&B also he became a real estate agent. Later he became the largest Real Estate Broker on the Island. His new entity is Island Real Estate. While he was purchasing his ticket, we began a conversation about the beauty of Holmes Beach. Out of the blue an employee Tom chimes in that his dad and uncle own condos on the island and these were for rent. These condos were at the Island Beach Club and sounded like a great place to rent.

Nothing in the world could have sounded nicer. Our beautiful granddaughter Ashley was two years and six months old and had been diagnosed with spinal meningitis. She was one of the lucky ones that caught it in time. Thank you, Ann for out thinking the doctor's assistant, Ashley now had to relearn how to walk. What a great idea; let's go to Florida. Frankie, Ann, the two girls at that time Ashley and Nicole, Papa and Signora. What a great time we had. On the second day Frankie and Ann took Nicole to Disney. We took care of Ashley for the day. My one claim to fame happened that day. Ashley took her first "new first steps" to Papa. Many tears flowed that afternoon; and what a great surprise for mom and dad when they arrived home that evening.

On this trip, Frank Davis took me around the Island and gave me some excellent advice. As of this date Frank has not made a real estate sale. I learned how everything is a trade off in Real Estate. The most important thing to remember in a resort town is that nearest to water is the criteria. Water is first then it's the location of the condo side versus front, up or down, elevator or not. Also a few more amenities could be considered. So, hello I purchased unit 103 in Gulf Sands for one hundred and five thousand dollars the following year I purchased 101 Gulf Sands and later sold it to son Frank and cousin Junior Paris at cost, ninety-eight thousand dollars. Later I purchased 206 at one hundred and ten thousand dollars. I now had two units.

I placed 103 and 206 in the hands of a rental agent. What a mistake; as a salesman, this guy was a disgrace. As of this time I was still with Allstate and the Travel Agency; of course, let's not forget one wife and two children, so I had to depend on a rental agent. Big mistake; I sold 103 for two hundred and fifty thousand dollars and after paying off the mortgage on 206, and I planned on using the overage on the purchase for another home rather than pay all the taxes on the profit. My "friend at Merrill Lynch" talked me into an investment of over sixty thousand dollars. This was all lost in two weeks. Lord only knows what his commission was. Of course, I hate him for life (the Sicilian side of me), but he is a nothing, because he lied to me. We went to court and he lied to me and the judge and my brand-new lawyer a dear friend was over matched. This was my guys first trial**, C'est La Vie.**

Onward and upwards (I heard this said once). I saw a beautiful two-family home on Clark Drive, about a block from the beach. This home was previously owned by the Pittsburg Pirates Baseball team, it was used for the ball players during spring training not bad, I think I paid two hundred and twenty-five thousand. Rentals were decent but I am still not satisfied with local rental agents. So, I sold for three hundred and fifty thousand dollars.

Every visit to Florida was a "would of, could of, and should of" saying. So, I had an urge and purchased 107 Cayman Cay. (I still own as of Sept. 24, 2016). This I purchased for two hundred and forty thousand dollars, this is across the street from 206 Gulf Sands and provides extra room for family. I was trying to show off to the grand kids. I bought this with no money down and took home equity loans on other property. It works but any extra money in rents must be allocated to pay the equity loans. This is very difficult for me I have a wee bit of a sickness with money. I do not gamble or drink yet I am always broke. Thanks for my beautiful wife that has kept our records for the first sixty years of marriage. If I ever cashed one of the checks I received over the years the bank would have refused it. She would cash my checks with my signature and deposit into her expense account. God, bless you sweet heart.

OMG! once again I did it again! I just turned eighty-five on the 7th of September and submitted an offer on the next-door unit in Gulf Sands. This unit 205 was owned by the same family since it was built in 1978. The daughters had it listed for a year at six hundred and fifty thousand dollars which it is way too high. No unit in our complex has broken the six hundred thousand dollars yet. I offered her five hundred and twenty-five thousand, and she countered at five hundred and forty thousand. Before I signed the papers, I asked my grandson the Financial Officer Nicholas, to run some "financials." It would be too difficult to show a positive cash flow at the end of each year. Also, I ran it by the family (The A team Frank and Carol). All things considered we decided not to purchase 205.

"But it's not over till it's over." Maybe in the next lifetime; for now, the family will have to make do with 2713 Ridgeway Ave., The Ski Haus, 206 Gulf Sands and 107 Cayman Cay. I was informed that my grandson Gregory (Ashley's husband) is on the Board of Director at St. Bonaventure in Olean, twenty miles from Ellicottville.

So as far as Ellicottville and the Ski Haus is concerned, "Ski Heil."

Borrelli Ski Haus

Ski Heil!

Ashley, Nick, and Nichole

Nick and Nichole

You guess who?

1970-1980: ALLSTATE

Same competitive chip on my shoulder; but the fun is gone. I have achieved all that I had hoped for. I think Allstate gave me all the recognition I needed. I no longer have need for the magic mirror. Everyone from the old neighborhood has complimented me on my achievements. Of course, my older friends have embellished all the stories. Without a doubt, the Army was the start to my adulthood; with the confidence needed to be a leader. No other kid from the Green Grass came close to the bar that was set. Now it's time to concentrate on family.

Frank entered St. Bonaventure as a freshman at age seventeen. Within a couple of years, he became a man with many friends. Frank can handle himself with kids from the neighborhood as well as the professional ones. This is a skill that not many people can master. Now Frank spends his time thinking he is a sports manager for Bryana. I do believe Frank thinks of himself as the guy in the "Gerry Mc Guire" movie.

Carol likewise finished her studies at Bryant and Stratton. Carol received a degree in business science. There was a great demand at Kodak and IBM and Bausch and Lomb. Carol decided on Kodak and worked in a lab at the research dept. of Kodak. Carol worked for some heavy-duty Doctors of Chemistry at Kodak. Carol has three children and three grandchildren. The three spend a great deal of time at "mima's" house. The kids know me as papa or it sounds like that anyway. They all know that I am the one that brings treats.

In Frank's senior year he met our lovely daughter in law Ann Edelman. We were introduced to Ann one weekend at Bonnies.

After dinner in Olean while walking to our car, Jean noted the chill and of course college students are not concerned with trivia like weather. So, signora offered Ann her Jacket. Jean is always prepared with extra clothes in cold weather. Both Jean and I were smitten with Ann. My father also was in love with Ann especially at Christmas Eve when he would cheat at cards. Sadly, dad passed away a few months prior to the wedding.

Next came Nicole, Ashley and Bryana; another book could be written about our love and laughter also sorrow that we enjoyed watching them grow into three beautiful young ladies.

Carol and David married a few years later; and then came Nicholas, Andrew and David. Also, the greatest, and never have I seen six cousins as close together in ages and as close as brother and sister. The best part of this closeness was the ages it seems that the girls are mated by age and grades in school. Nicole was the oldest and she immediately became the "boss." Bryanna became the self-proclaimed "favorite grandchild." Ashley and Andrew filled the bill of "middle children." David as the youngest

Borrelli to Coach at World Cup Lacrosse Festival

Coach Borrelli To Coach DI Elite Team

Head Coach Bryana Borrelli

July 14, 2017

LOUDONVILLE, N.Y. - Women's Lacrosse Head Coach Bryana Borrelli will lead the U19 Elite team at the World Lacrosse Cup Festival at the Surrey Sports Park in Guildford, England. Borrelli and the team will play four days of competition in the hopes of taking the World Cup Lacrosse Festival Championship title.

"To experience the game at an international level is a very special thing, said Borrelli. "I am honored and grateful to have the opportunity to lead a team overseas."

The World Cup Lacrosse Festival will take place during the FIL Rathbones Women's Lacrosse World Cup, which will also be played at Surrey Sports Park. Borrelli's squad will play their first day of competition on Monday, July 17. While on the trip, the team will take a tour of Windsor Palace.

The final day of the festival is Friday, July 21 will the championship and consolation games taking place. The 2017 FIL Rathbones World Cup Championship will take place on Saturday, July 22 so the team will be able to go to the championship before heading back to the United States on Sunday, July 23.

along with Bryanna was a wee bit different; like the youngest are supposed to be. Frank or "Dan Mc quire" had his "jock" Bryana the lacrosse player and Div. I coach.

It was so much fun watching the grandkids grow. We never missed a ball game, cheerleading or any other school event; to me education is the most important part of growing up. I am so proud of all six children, having completed college plus. Thank God, I could share in all these education accomplishments; and to a small part was able to contribute.

Although I grew up alone, I had many cousins. To most children cousins are their first and best friends. Grandpa and grandma had nine children so I had many cousins. All children must visit grandpa's house [Italian families for sure] so living with Grandpa I was able to get to see and know all my cousins. I had favorites my cousin Frank "Ike" Paris the best baseball player in the world [to me anyway]. When Ike went into the service in WWII he gave me all his old baseball jerseys. When he returned from the war in 1945 he also gave me a pair of binoculars taken from a Japanese sniper. I cherished these for sixty years and wish whoever borrowed them will please return them. Cousin Ike was also wounded on one of the Pacific Islands. No war is fun but I cannot imagine how rugged it must have been to be involved in jungle warfare. Cousin Ferdinand Carson was a top turret gunner on a B17 Bomber and he was shot down over Germany. Fern was a POW for a long while and I am sure that took its toll. Fern was also my favorite cousin. Fern was also given a purple heart for his wounds.

My cousins Rose Carson and Delores Speciale were the two most beautiful girls in the world. (At least I thought so) My friend "Snacky" had a cousin Jack Stevens that he was close to; I also thought Jack was "cool" wow, he played drums. Jack was a great drummer of that time, he played drums and vibes. I am not sure of the reason but Jack purchased a set of vibes and had them stored at Snack's house. Anna, one of my favorite surrogate moms was an immaculate housekeeper. One day, Anna noticed that the vibes were dusty; so, she proceeded to wipe all the pipes with her favorite dust rag. Jack arrived one afternoon and almost fainted; I guess there is a special way to dust or wipe these bright tubes. **C'est la vie.**

Wherever there are cousins there are uncle and aunts. I loved each of my aunts and uncles. My aunt Teresa lived with us for years. She would take me downtown whenever she was shop lifting. If caught she would plead with the store guard that she was poor and she had this little boy. Enough said about that issue. Next my Aunt Angie. She was divorced but her husband uncle Charlie was on Sabbatical in prison. He once sent home the most beautiful sailboat made while in prison. It was finished over the wooden sides with thousands of burned out book matches. It was magnificent.

My first week in the Army I read an article; how the "Federals" raided a still in upstate New York. This was the largest still ever seen, it made thousands of gallons of alcohol. It was said that they were cheating the tax people of thousands of dollars a day in lost revenue. **Autres temps, autres moeurs**

Uncles and aunts have a paternal love for nephews and nieces. They are real surrogate mothers and fathers. Aunt Maggie I loved because she was frail and she did a heck of a great job with her children. She was thought to be dead and was covered for the next process. Someone noticed a breath and she came through for another 20 years.

My Aunt Maggie's six children were put into foster homes.

Her sisters had 6 to 9 children of their own and this was during the depression of the 1930's hence "the Foster Home" but all of life became normal when all returned together. Also, I remembered Uncle John would go outdoors at New Year's Eve, "drunk" and shoot off a shotgun.

My Aunt Jennie with the 9 children were convinced that she was my favorite aunt. She was correct; man, cold she makes Easter cookies and pies. Her husband uncle Louie worked at Richardson Root Beer. We always had syrup home; just mix with cold water and it is a great drink especially the orange.

They even had a load of chickens in their back yards. We always had fresh eggs during the war.

Aunt Mary was also a great baker mostly pies. She had three great sons that were older and bigger but would let me play catch with them. They were good but a wee bit too Americanized. My Aunt Mary's husband was killed in WWI. There was a large Cannon in front of the American Legion Post on Dewey Ave, named after him.

Uncle Peter wounded by Gas in WWI and spent his whole life up to 1944 in a nursing home. He was laid out in death in my bedroom at home.

Uncle Tony "wolf" was a "downtown" guy. He loved to gamble and was an excellent barber. He was always broke. I remember him taking me to the boxing gym every week and then the steam baths after. He was an amateur boxer and professional barber. Many doctors and businessmen down town were his clients. Also, all the Hi rollers, this included the man; Mikey Troy. Mike was big, he loved my uncle, they seemed to have a common denominator. I also remember seeing Uncle Tony come home and steal a few coins from grandpa's pockets. You could tell when he lost he would come home and punch the walls and swear.

Uncle Louie "Jock" my favorite, he was rich and handsome. Uncle Louis could not read or write. But he could count to 21 for Black Jack. Uncle Louie was as sharp as my dad both were handsome as a movie star. Rumor had it that he had a ton of women admirers. Later he married my Aunt Mary she was a teacher in Mt. Morris and her family were well known. Her family did not want anything to do with my uncle; they all thought of him as a womanizer. This was so far from the truth; uncle was as close as I have ever seen any couple. Each year he would sport a new Coupe' Chevy. And they were called coupe' not coup. Both would come to our house to see Grandpa and eat; then off to Aunt Mary's house for pie deserts. On every trip, I would admire the three-ct. diamond he wore on his pinkie; won in a crap game. Uncle was drafted not only could he not read but he was left handed. A Sgt. tried to make him do all things righty even throwing a grenade. After about 35 days he was given a discharge. He was so proud of this that he joined the American Legion. He qualified for his thirty-day service. The largest and best American legion was on University Ave. Post #1182; about ten years later Uncle Louie became President of the Post.

He was the best barber in Lima, (he was the only one) for thirty years and his back room had a magnificent pool table. This of course made into a crap table. When Mike Troy got closed in Rochester the games began in Louie's Barber shop. I mean big games. Along about these years they bought a home on Conesus Lake and a fourteen-room home on Main Street in Mt. Morris. This home had antiques worth over a million dollars. Uncle Louie also owned with a partner a lot of their Main Street. When Aunt Mary became ill she was hospitalized for an extended time.

My uncle was a lost soul first he was devoted to his wife and now he was not able to fill out various forms. My cousin Genevieve left the convent a few years earlier and was visiting uncle with her new husband Don. My uncle met them at the door unshaven and disheveled never ever is this dapper Uncle Louis. The family was told that he gave her a bag of coins and; we were told "my husband is an expert on coins and will determine the value." Here we go again first a watch for confirmation now a gorgeous ring. Uncle then says take this ring and give it to Frank. We have six Franks in the family I am the only Borrelli. "Jay" did exactly what she was told, that's all she was given. The ring was brought not to Frank Paris or Frank Carson and not to me as promised over a hundred times. But to Frank Barber my cousin. Frank never wore the ring. I never forgot the promise. Next Uncle Louie proceeds after Jay left to go up to the attic very distraught that he was unable to fill out his cars registration. He committed suicide. One week later my aunt died. Upon the suicide, all assets went to his wife Mary. There was no will "that we know of." When Mary died all her assets went to her family at least two million or more. This is the family that had nothing to do with Uncle Louie. The proceeds from the home, the business, the seventeen-room house and the summer home all were given to her family. **C'est la vie.** I think in retrospect; a lawyer should have been consulted. I think Uncle Tony punched out a few walls. Jay came to our house and gave my dad about ten dollars in change and said; "here is your share of all the coins. Don figured what they were worth." OMG, my father jumps off the chair, picks up the bag of coins and throws all the coins outside in the snow. He begins to swear and says my brother was just buried today and you come here with your bag of coins, get the hell out of here and take those coins in the snow back with you. "At a boy dad give them hell."

Sadly, as you grow older and meet different kids at school or neighborhood friends all will scatter as they get older and go off to college and then marry. I give that another; **Autres temps autres moeurs**.

In our time, slowly but surely you will almost always lose contact with your cousins. The only time in most cases you will see them is at funerals and weddings. It is possible not even then. To prove a point about cousins being close for life; yesterday I went to a wake for Domenic "Moose" Borrelli. Most people there were in their sixties or older. Moose was ninety and some of his age group was there. Other members of the Parkers semi football team post WWII.

OMG this was truly a celebration of life. Moose was a great natural athlete, I remember him well, having a problem with his lower jaw, he improvised a mask for his football helmet. Dom screwed on to the front of the helmet a softball baseball catcher's mask. He was fifty years ahead of the curve. Every Saturday at our sandlot games Dom loaned me his helmet. This was the only equipment I wore; it was great since I was a center and defense from high schools were taught to slap the centers head each time the ball was centered. In anticipation of this slap or punch the center was supposed to get apprehensive and make a bad center.

The Borrelli's at the funeral were all related to the Giuliano, Catallo, Diponzio and Bonanza also Gioia and Rotella. Never in my eighty-five years have I seen anything like this. So many older people remembered me, the kid with no mother. They all spoke so kindly of my dad Frank, Butch, Sullivan Borrelli. Those were his four names and all were used daily. The Butch I understood but I never could figure the Sullivan or Sully thing. I know he was a contest marathon dancer and they may have used some pseudo Irish names.

My mentor and I.

Memories with Billy Benedict. I found out at lunch today that Bill lost his mom at age five ... I never knew that. I realized I was fortunate in another strange way. Most parents in our day spoke very little English; but to hear all the "broken English "as we called it was all we heard and laughed with them not at them. It really was a thing of beauty. Because of this along with limited knowledge of customs; most neighborhood kids did not "call upon" friends in the usual way; especially during Sunday Dinner. The drill was to line up on the walks in front of the home. And all yell for; Snacky, Butch, Chuchie or Spaghetti etc. "can you come out and play we need another guy for football or another game."

These are actual names; one day several of us ventured over the subway bridge to number 30 school areas. We needed a strong kid for football. When we arrived at his home we began to shout for "Spaghetti." "Can you come out we need a full back." After several minutes, his mom came out to reprimand us.

In a beautiful broken English voice, she shouted; "why ya calla my son spaghetti"? He has a niceah name his namea isa called Ralphieee." ... Words cannot do justice to the sound of these beautiful words coming out of this dear lady. You must use your imagination; close your eyes and try to hear her. It's been over 70 years and I can still hear her. It was a beautiful thing.

This woman raised four children during the depression and all graduated high school. A piece of cake today for most kids, still to this day we do not have 100% completion. These were the Immigrants of the turn of the 20th century. A lot of guts and love did wonders for a wage earner of maybe fifty cents an hour.

Having so many surrogate mothers I never had to call any of my friends, especially Snacky Nacca. I loved his mother Anna. I can still see her walking a mile a minute from Barbato's grocery store. I always rang the bell and was invited in to wait inside or join them in dinner. Autres temps-autres moeurs.

Today I became so involved in conversations that I forgot all about Jean at the hair dresser. I dropped her off at 3:20 and promised to be back by four pm. Suddenly I look at the entrance and see Bill Benedict at the door with his hand up making a motion like a talking parrot. Oh, Oh, I am in trouble now it's after five pm. I drove to Linda's house our hairdresser; only to find a post it notes on the door. "Frank, I took Jean home." I arrived home to a silent wife but a very verbal daughter Carol trying to get the burnt roast out of the oven. Then they both proceeded to beat on me.

None of the Borrelli's were related to me in fact, I have no idea if any of my cousins are still alive. I am sure that I now have achieved all that I was capable of. I provided for my wife and my family. To quote from Sinatra "Idid it my way." There are some regrets in hind sight. There always will be a "Monday morning quarterback" that can-do things differently. What I would not do differently is the family closeness. I like to think that I and Signora had a hand in that. I have never seen a family as close to ours especially that they have some old-world customs. Kissing and hugs regardless of how old we all are.

Of the six grandkids Nicole, Nicholas, Ashley and David are now married. Andrew seems smitten and Bryana the baby is the only one out of town. We are so proud of her a Division one head coach at Sienna College. Nicholas a senior financial officer, Nicole and Ashley started their own "spinning studio." David has started his company doing resurfacing of driveways and plowing. Andrew must have a few of my genes he is a salesman for ADP,a payroll and employee resources company. This is one tough sell, "cold calls." Been there done that and was terrible at it.

How lucky are we to have five great grand babies OMG! I like to just stare at them any chance I get? Too bad I cannot hug and play as their grandparents do. Again, a for sure **C'est la vie**; it's time for the grandparents to get the enjoyment meant for them.

Both, Jean and I experienced it but our parents did not. I started to write the next sentence and got the weirdest feeling in my stomach. OMG! I do believe our parents are watching "Carli" Ann and Frankie and the whole Clan.

The cutest thing was the cousin's day at Deanna's home all five of the Great grandbabies. All five second cousins had a picnic and photo shoot. This is an accumulation of all things I ever wanted rolled into the five second cousins. It appears that these cousins will continue our legacy.

"Already Two Gatherings".

New Year's Eve celebration Dec. 31, 2016

This is last of the green grass boys on New Year's Eve. Nick

My children, Frank and Carol

Visco, Jimmy Barbato, Billy Benedict and myself. We have celebrated together for over sixty years. We started the custom

with as many as twenty singles and twenty with female friends or wives. What wonderful memories we have of those times with our neighbor- hood friends.

During the past sixty years, we were great friends and remain friends. We enjoyed the good in each of the members and made light of the mistakes that were made by some. "Only God is perfect".

In our youth, we all went "Prime Time" for New Year's Eve, Dinner at nine or ten and Midnight mass at St. Anthony'sChurch. Kisses and more food and more celebration till three or four AM. Now we dine at six or seven and home by eight to the comfort of the recliner to view the NYC celebration on TV; providing we can stay awake till midnight.

This holiday January 1, 2017, we hit the jackpot and lottery all in one. What we wanted to see came true to life. Frankie and Ann, Nicole and Jarrett with the two babies went to the ski Haus. In the front unit, Little David and Julie with Olivia; also, Andrew and his friend Brittany also spent the eve there. Nicholas and Deanna with Noah and Tyler were committed. This is what we had hoped for; cousins together and close. That made the expense of the addition- al home worth every penny we spend on it.

Now the happenings that make our lives complete. New Year's Eve our whole family called at midnight to wish us a Happy New Year.

Sunday morning New Year's Day, Jean wakes up and starts a large pot of sauce. She added to the sauce ten links of sausage and two dozen meat balls.

Nine AM, Carol called and wished us a Happy New Year.Next "what you all doing today;" my response "nothing, moms making a pot of sauce. "Good we will be over this afternoon.

Ten AM, Frank and Ann called, same old what are you doing thing "Good we will be over this afternoon."

Eleven AM, Nicholas and Deanna with the two boys. Same drill and glad to have a gathering.

This is what I prayed for since boyhood. I believe we have exceeded my expectations

Our Family Tree

Grand Parents
Francesco Borrelli- born 1872-- died 1944, married Teresa Bovenzi born 1872 died 1942

Parents
Frank Peter Borrelli born 1910 died 1973, married Josephine Cartisano born 1911 died 1980

Francis Joseph Borrelli born 1931, married Jean Tese 1932

Our Son
Francis L. Borrelli born 11-6-1954, married Ann Edelman born 1956

His Children and our Grand children
Nichole 7-17-82 married Jerrit Brannigan
Ashly 1-28-84 married Gregory Bryla
Bryana 7-10-88 single

His Grand Children and our Great Grandchildren
Francesa 4-11-2013 Antonia 1-12-2016

Our Daughter
Carol Ann Borrelli born 1956, married Dave Cavalieri born 1956

Her Children our Grand children
Nicholas 5-20-83 married Deanna Simonetti 10-09-83
Andrew 10-16-84 single
David 4-1-87 married Julie Richiuso 8-13-86

Her Grand Children and our Great Grandchildren
Noah 4-14-2014 Tyler 9-16-15 Olivia 7-6-2016

In 1998, I put Allstate behind me and retired to a new role. I am now a champion gopher; "Papa if you are near BJ's can you pick up some diapers?" Or Dad," if you go By BJ's I can use some coffee." Of course, Carol Ann is a coffee snob.

About the Author

The Book Speaks for Itself and In My Own Words.

We are all given a chance in life to attack life, stay dormant, or retreat. My options were to sulk, feel sorry for myself or attack life. My father was a born talker that could charm or sell a person the Brooklyn Bridge. I hung with him for 16 years and learned all his habits. I honestly can say I was very proud of him and tried to emulate on his moves. This is where I believe that genes can have an important part in our character.

For whatever its worth I believe I achieved all that was possible with the limited education and a lot of [as my son Frank says] "street smarts."

None of what I accomplished could be possible without my wife Jean. Two children in diapers and I am out of the house from five AM and return after midnight. But I was always home for supper and sometimes a park picnic for supper. And take this literary I was in our bed every night. Divorce was never an option!

Can you imagine; two children in diapers a two-bed room apartment on Smith St. no money in the bank and telling your wife you are going to open a jewelry store? We were crazy, no question about that. That is Love carried to the nth degree. Jean never questioned me and had confidence that one cannot measure. She would always say "I am your best friend."

Love you my 16-year-old "Beastie Baby" from Charlotte Beach.

65901331R00111

Made in the USA
Lexington, KY
28 July 2017